JOHN HADAMUSCIN'S

Home for Christmas

Decorating, Cooking, Entertaining, and Giving

Photographs by Randy O'Rourke

Harmony Books   New York

*For my family and friends, the people who always make my holidays special.
I will be thinking of you at Christmastime as a thousand memories come rushing back.*

*And for Diane Cleaver, friend and agent extraordinaire—you will always
be an inspiration! Thanks for eight books together!*

Design by Ken Sansone

Copyright © 1995 by John Hadamuscin
Photographs copyright © 1995 by Randy O'Rourke

Published by Harmony Books, a division of Crown Publishers, Inc.,
201 East 50th Street, New York, New York 10022.
Member of the Crown Publishing Group.

Random House, Inc. New York, Toronto, London, Sydney, Auckland
Harmony and colophon are trademarks of Crown Publishers, Inc.
Manufactured in China

LIBRARY OF CONGRESS CATALOGING-IN-PUBLICATION DATA

Hadamuscin, John.

John Hadamuscin's home for Christmas : decorating, cooking,
entertaining, and giving / photographs by Randy O'Rourke.—1st ed.

Includes index.

1. Christmas cookery. 2. Christmas decorations.
3. Entertaining. I. Title. II. Title: Home for Christmas
TX739.2.C45H33   1995
641.5'68—dc20 95-6992
CIP

ISBN 0-517-70180-4

10 9 8 7 6 5 4 3 2 1
FIRST EDITION

Contents

Christmastime

There is that moment every year when one second I feel I'm a mature-acting adult going about the world in a sensible, orderly way and the very next second I'm a child again, dreaming of magic and wonders. It can be as simple as a snowflake, the first Christmas song, the first card, wreaths in windows, or the first ringing Salvation Army bell. It is the start of the most special season of the year.

There is no place like home for Christmas, and for most of us, even though we now have our own homes, families, and friends, "home" is forever embedded in our minds as the place where we grew up.

At our house, right after Thanksgiving we

would get started. There was much to be done—plum puddings, fruitcakes, cranberry relish, cookies all had to be made in advance. Gifts of nature were gathered to make wreaths of greens and pinecones and other ornaments. Folks would be stopping by, so we always had a small homemade gift to offer.

The time would zoom by and there it was—Christmas Eve, the day we kids waited for all year. In the early evening we would go to church, where my brothers and I always had a part in the Christmas pageant. The church was filled with candles, and two tall trees were decorated with symbols of our Lutheran holiday traditions. Then it was home for a supper of seafood soup if we were lucky and as many cookies as we could eat. Then back to church for the candlelight service. I remember the carols, the chimes, and the voices. I can still feel and see the tears as we all sang "Silent Night" together at the end of the service. It's as if it were only a moment ago.

And then came the longest night of the year as the temperature dipped below freezing and soft drifts of snow and chains of icicles formed.

There was not much sleep as we lay wrapped in wool blankets and quilts; our thoughts were of tomorrow. I can remember how hard my heart pounded—it was a true and believing heart. I felt a thrill, like no other time or season.

On Christmas morning we were not allowed downstairs until we were called—Dad was already out in the barn milking cows and feeding the chickens and pigs and Mom was in the kitchen preparing for the day's events. But I could hear and smell Christmas. At last we would be called downstairs to a day filled with magic and wonder, a day you hoped would never end. Each year there would be a wonderful gift, such as my first bike or my beloved horse Maisie, and the house would be filled with my grandmothers and many other relatives and friends. And scents of Christmases were everywhere—the tree,

oranges, mulled cider, the roasting of turkey or country ham, biscuits, and cakes and pies. And it was a day of eating well. If Christmas was the slowest day to come along, it was the fastest day ever to go by.

Christmas is the combination of many things—home, family, friends, food, music, laughter, customs, traditions, and goodwill, a time of sharing and remembering. It is layered in memories, and for me, each Christmas memory is enough to last a lifetime. I remember each and every Christmas as if it were yesterday. And as the magic of each Christmas passes and fades away, it will always reappear next year, for that is the promise of Christmas.

John

Walnut Hill, Christmas 1995

Gifts from the Kitchen

Spiced Orange Curd

Honey-Herb Vinegar

Brandied Pears with Berries

Honey-Apricot Jam

Bourbon Jelly

Cranberry-Port Conserve

Cherry Ketchup

Christmastime Marmalade

Garlicky Herbed Olives

My New Favorite Plum Pudding

Golden Dried Fruitcake

Swedish Glögg

In my travels around the country, readers who've come to my signings and lectures have brought me some extraordinary gifts: homemade chutneys and jams, a handwritten book of family recipes brought from the Old World, homegrown and dried shuck beans, and even a handmade Santa or two. One lovely lady, Hermine Kelty, who refers to herself as my "senior citizen groupie," even brought me a family cookie recipe along with the cutter to use for making them.

These simple gifts mean a great deal to me. They're an expression of caring and sharing and, let's face it, that's what Christmas is all about. Here are some of the gifts that I like to give.

Spiced Orange Curd
* * *
MAKES 4 HALF-PINTS

This golden, creamy spread is just wonderful slathered onto a toasted English muffin. I like to package it in little half-pint jars tied up with twine or gauzy gold ribbon, with a dried orange slice (page 44) and a cinnamon stick tied into the bow.

1 teaspoon whole cloves
1 small cinnamon stick, broken into 3 or 4
  pieces
Juice and grated rind of 6 large juice
  oranges
15 large eggs

3 cups sugar
1½ cups (3 sticks) unsalted butter,
   softened

1. Tie the spices up in cheesecloth or a coffee filter. Place the spice bag and orange juice in a medium, heavy saucepan and place over medium heat. Bring the mixture to a simmer and cook for 2 minutes. Remove from the heat and let stand 1 hour.

2. Discard the spice bag and pour the juice into a blender or the bowl of a food processor fitted with the steel chopping blade. (Don't wash the pan yet.) Add the eggs, sugar, and butter and process until very smooth.

3. Transfer the mixture to the saucepan, stir in the orange rind, and place the pan over low heat. Cook, whisking frequently to keep the mixture smooth, until the mixture is thickened to a puddinglike consistency, about 10 minutes (it will thicken more when cooled).

4. Spoon the orange curd into 4 half-pint jars, cover, and store in the refrigerator.

Honey-Herb Vinegar

* * *

MAKES 2 PINTS

This unusual vinegar makes a great quick salad dressing when mixed with a fruity olive oil. It's also good on steamed vegetables.

3 cups white wine vinegar
1½ cups dry white wine
¾ cup honey
2 shallots, peeled and halved lengthwise

2 sprigs thyme
2 sprigs rosemary
2 2-inch strips lemon peel, white pith
   removed

1. In a medium saucepan, combine the vinegar, white wine, and honey and place over medium-low heat. Bring to a simmer, reduce heat to low, and simmer gently for 20 minutes. Add the shallots and continue simmering for 15 minutes.

2. Have ready 2 sterilized pint bottles. Place 2 shallot halves, a sprig each of thyme and rosemary, and a strip of lemon peel in each bottle. Pour the vinegar mixture into the bottles, then seal the bottles. Store in a cool place.

Honey-Herb Vinegar is packaged in an assortment of old and new bottles with new corks and colorful ribbons.

Jars of brandied pears are topped with metallic tissue paper and tied with narrow ribbons.

Brandied Pears with Berries

* * *

MAKES 4 QUARTS

*D*elicious with a scoop of French vanilla ice cream, with a spice cookie alongside.

1¾ cups sugar
4 cinnamon sticks
24 ripe, firm Seckel pears (about 6½ pounds)
½ pint raspberries
2 pints brandy, approximately

1. Place 4 quarts water, the sugar, and cinnamon sticks in a large, heavy saucepan. Peel the pears, leaving the stems on, and immediately place each one into the pan to prevent browning.

2. Place the pan over medium heat and bring the mixture to a simmer. Reduce the heat to low and simmer until the pears are tender but not mushy, 15 to 20 minutes.

3. Divide half the pears among 4 sterilized quart jars, then divide half the berries among the jars on top of the pears. Repeat with the remaining fruit, then tuck a cinnamon stick into each jar.

4. Carefully pour the syrup from the pan into the jars, dividing it evenly. Add enough brandy to each jar, cover the pears, then seal the jars with their lids. Turn the jars over a few times to combine the syrup and brandy. Allow to cool, then store the jars in a cool place (or refrigerate) for at least 2 weeks before using.

Honey-Apricot Jam

* * *

MAKES 4 HALF-PINTS

*I*t's nice to have a few easy recipes on hand that quickly transform kitchen staples into much more than the sum of the parts. Here, without any extra shopping and with very little work, is one of those recipes. This is wonderful on whole wheat toast.

2 cups coarsely chopped dried apricots
1¼ cups water
¼ cup lemon juice
½ teaspoon ground cinnamon
½ teaspoon ground ginger
½ teaspoon grated nutmeg
1 cup honey

1. Combine the apricots, water, lemon juice, and spices in a medium saucepan and place over medium-high heat. Bring to a simmer and cook 5 minutes, then reduce the heat to medium-low and continue simmering, stirring occasionally, until the apricots are very tender and almost all the liquid is absorbed, about 20 minutes.

A FEW NOTES ON CANNING

*

- Always wash jars and lids well and sterilize them by boiling for 15 minutes just before using. Recycling jars is fine, but always use new lids.
- Items with low acidity should be processed in a boiling water bath. Place the sealed jars 1 inch apart on a rack in a large kettle. Pour warm water into the kettle to cover the jars by 2 inches and gradually bring the water to a boil. Boil half-pint jars for 10 minutes, pint jars for 15 minutes. Remove the jars with tongs and allow to cool gradually before labeling and storing.

2. Stir in the honey and return the mixture to a simmer. Cook, stirring frequently to prevent sticking, until the mixture reaches a thick jamlike consistency, about 10 minutes (the jam will thicken more when it cools). Spoon the jam into 4 half-pint jars, seal, and process in a boiling water bath (above) for 10 minutes. Cool the jars on a wire rack and store in a cool place.

Bourbon Jelly

* * *

MAKES 4 HALF-PINTS

*U*nusual and very easy to make—with no extra trips to the store to hunt for odd ingredients—this is a nice condiment to serve with country ham, smoked turkey, or smoked pork chops. The jelly can be made with Scotch or Irish whiskey as well.

The jars at right were topped with squares of printed tissue and tied with twine, then sprigs of fresh boxwood were tucked into the bows. The labels were cut out of used brown paper grocery bags with pinking shears.

2 envelopes (2 tablespoons) unflavored
   gelatin
$2\frac{2}{3}$ cups water
$\frac{2}{3}$ cup sugar
$\frac{2}{3}$ cup strained orange juice
$1\frac{1}{3}$ cups Bourbon whiskey

1. In a medium bowl, combine the gelatin with $1\frac{1}{3}$ cups water, stirring to soften the gelatin. Place the remaining water in a small saucepan and bring to a boil. Stir the boiling water into the gelatin mixture and stir until the gelatin is dissolved. Add the sugar and stir until it is dissolved.

2. Add the orange juice and Bourbon, stirring until the mixture is well blended. Spoon the mixture into 4 sterilized half-pint jars and seal. Cool to room temperature, then store in the refrigerator.

Cranberry-Port Conserve

* * *

MAKES ABOUT 4 PINTS

A heady but elegant condiment, especially good with ham, duck, or even goose.

2 cups ruby port
2 cups sugar
2 cups golden raisins
1 teaspoon grated orange rind
6 cups (2 12-ounce bags) cranberries

1. Combine the port and sugar in a medium saucepan, place over medium-high heat, and stir until the sugar is dissolved and the mixture comes to a simmer. Stir in the raisins and orange rind, reduce the heat, and simmer for 5 minutes.

2. Add the cranberries, bring the mixture to a simmer again, and cook, stirring occasionally, until all the berries pop and the liquid is syrupy, about 10 minutes.

Jars of Cherry Ketchup, Spiced Orange Curd, and Christmastime Marmalade are decorated to suggest the contents before being packed together in a basket.

3. Transfer the mixture into sterilized pint jars and seal the lids. Allow the jars to cool, then store in a cool place.

Cherry Ketchup

* * *

MAKES ABOUT 7 HALF-PINTS

I like to make this unusual condiment to use as gifts as well as for serving with Currant-Glazed Country Ham (page 58)—it's always a nice surprise to have the flavor of cherries at this time of year. The secret (unless, of course, you make the ketchup during cherry season) is using frozen and canned cherries, which are available in the supermarket all year long.

10 whole allspice berries
10 whole cloves
2 cinnamon sticks, broken into 1-inch pieces
6¾ cups (2 12-ounce bags) frozen sweet cherries, thawed
3 cups (2 16-ounce cans, drained) sour cherries
1 large onion, coarsely chopped
2 garlic cloves, chopped
1 cup firmly packed light brown sugar
1 cup granulated sugar
1¼ cups white vinegar
½ teaspoon almond extract

1. Tie the spices up in a 4-inch square of cheesecloth and place them and all the remaining ingredients except the almond extract in a large, heavy saucepan. Place the pan over medium-high heat and bring the mixture to a boil, stirring frequently to prevent sticking.

2. Reduce the heat to low and simmer, stirring occasionally, until the syrup has thickened, 45 to 50 minutes. Remove the pan from the heat, remove the spice bag, and stir in the extract.

3. In batches, transfer the mixture to the bowl of a food processor fitted with the steel chopping blade and process until almost smooth. Spoon the ketchup into 7 half-pint jars, seal, and process in a boiling water bath (page 9) for 10 minutes. Allow the jars to cool, then store in a cool place.

Christmastime Marmalade

* * *

MAKES 7 HALF-PINTS

It's no secret that I'm a big fan of cranberries in any shape or form, so I'm sneaking in another recipe that features them. Here they add color and zing to a traditional citrus marmalade. Try this for breakfast or at teatime, spread onto scones or toasted grainy bread.

1 orange
1 lemon
1 grapefruit (preferably red)
2¾ cups water
5½ cups sugar
3 cups (1 12-ounce bag) cranberries
¼ teaspoon ground cloves

1. Slice the stem ends off the citrus fruits, then cut the lemon and orange into 6 wedges and the grapefruit into 8 wedges. Remove any seeds and cut the fruit, skin and all, crosswise into paper-thin slices (it's okay if the flesh falls apart; it will cook down anyway).

2. In a heavy, medium saucepan, combine the pared fruit with the water and place over medium-high heat. Bring to a boil, reduce the heat to low, and simmer gently until the fruit peel begins to become tender, 45 to 50 minutes.

3. Stir in the sugar and cranberries and bring to a simmer again. Simmer until the marmalade is thickened and the fruit peel is quite tender, about 20 minutes. Stir in the cloves. Spoon the marmalade into 7 sterilized half-pint jars, seal, and store in a cool place.

For packaging boxed gifts, I like to recycle brown grocery bags and the classifieds from the Sunday paper. Binder's twine, plaid ribbons, little sprigs of greenery and berries, and tiny pinecones add the finishing touches.

The addition of garlic and herbs to rejarred store-bought olives transforms them into a flavorful gift.

Garlicky Herbed Olives

* * *

MAKES 2 PINTS

This simple method really enhances the so-so flavor of domestic store-bought olives. Fresh herbs are available more and more in larger supermarkets, so by all means use them.

> *4 7-ounce jars whole green olives*
> *4 large garlic cloves, crushed*
> *4 2-inch strips lemon peel*
> *2 sprigs each rosemary, thyme, and oregano*
> *1 teaspoon hot red pepper flakes*
> *White wine vinegar*

1. Drain the olives, reserving the brine, and divide them between 2 sterilized pint jars. Tuck 2 garlic cloves, 2 strips of lemon peel, and a sprig of each herb into each of the jars. Sprinkle ½ teaspoon pepper flakes into each jar, then pour the reserved brine over the olives, covering them

completely. Add white wine vinegar if necessary to cover the olives.

2. Seal the jars and store the olives in the refrigerator for at least a week, turning the jars every few days to allow the flavors to mellow.

My New Favorite Plum Pudding

* * *

MAKES ONE 2-QUART PUDDING
OR FOUR 1-PINT PUDDINGS

Christmas can't go by in my house without making—and eating—a rich, aromatic plum pudding, but I'm finding of late that I enjoy it more after a light meal rather than as dessert after a big Christmas dinner. A plum pudding recipe was included in my very first book, *The Holidays*; this recipe is a somewhat lightened version of that one.

> *1½ cups golden raisins*
> *1½ cups dried cranberries or currants*
> *1 cup chopped dried apricots*
> *3 large baking apples, pared and diced*
> *2 tablespoons finely chopped gingerroot*
> *½ cup brandy*
> *Juice and grated rind of 1 orange*
> *1½ cups unbleached all-purpose flour*
> *1 teaspoon baking powder*
> *1 teaspoon salt*
> *2 teaspoons ground cinnamon*
> *2 teaspoons ground ginger*
> *1 teaspoon ground cloves*
> *½ teaspoon grated nutmeg*
> *½ cup chopped candied orange peel*
> *½ cup chopped candied lemon peel*

1 cup sliced almonds
1½ cups fine dry bread crumbs
1¼ cups firmly packed dark brown sugar
1 cup vegetable shortening
4 large eggs, lightly beaten

1. In a mixing bowl, combine the raisins, cranberries or currants, apricots, apples, ginger, brandy, and orange juice and rind and stir well. Cover the bowl and let stand 1 hour.

2. In a separate large bowl, sift together the flour, baking powder, salt, and spices. Combine the fruit mixture, the orange and lemon peels, and the almonds with the flour mixture and toss until the fruit is coated. Stir in the bread crumbs.

3. In a separate mixing bowl, cream the sugar and shortening together, then beat in the eggs. Add this mixture to the large bowl and mix well, making a very stiff batter.

4. Grease a 2-quart pudding mold (or other round 2-quart pan) or 4 pint molds very well, then spoon the batter into it. Cover the mold tightly with its lid (or if using a lidless pan, use well-greased wax paper covered with aluminum foil tied tightly with kitchen twine). Place the mold in a large kettle and pour hot water into the kettle to come about ¾ of the way up the side of the mold.

5. Cover the pot and steam the pudding over medium heat for 8 hours (6 hours for the smaller puddings), adding hot water as needed.

6. When the pudding is done, remove the mold from the pot and allow to cool to room temperature, then refrigerate the pudding, stored in the covered mold, for a minimum of 4 weeks. To use

Every year on Thanksgiving weekend I make several plum puddings—a few for giving and one for myself. This pudding is served on an antique cake stand and decorated with lemon leaves and kumquats.

the puddings as gifts, unmold the puddings and wrap them tightly in cellophane tied with ribbon.

7. To serve, allow the pudding to come to room temperature, then resteam it again for 1 hour. (Unmolded gift puddings can be wrapped tightly in foil and reheated in a slow oven.) Unmold the pudding onto a heatproof serving dish.

Golden Dried Fruitcake

✳ ✳ ✳

MAKES TWO 8½ X 4½-INCH
LOAVES

Forget all the "haha, fruitcake" jokes and stories that those smarties like to spread around. This version of fruitcake will not be passed on from year to year untouched as those cakes in the stories and jokes are. My favorite way of serving it is in small slices that have been toasted, then topped with a scoop of vanilla ice cream and some toasted slivered almonds.

1 cup golden raisins
¾ cup chopped dried apricots
1 cup chopped dried apples
¾ cup chopped dried pineapple
½ cup chopped candied orange peel
2 cups blanched almonds
1 cup brandy
1½ cups (3 sticks) unsalted butter, melted
2 cups granulated sugar
½ cup firmly packed light brown sugar
8 large eggs, separated
1 teaspoon vanilla extract
1 teaspoon almond extract
Grated rind of 1 orange
4 cups unbleached all-purpose flour
2 teaspoons baking powder
1 teaspoon salt
1 teaspoon grated nutmeg
½ teaspoon ground cloves

1. In a heavy, medium saucepan, combine the raisins, apricots, apples, pineapple, candied orange peel, and almonds with ¾ cup of the brandy. Place over medium heat, bring the brandy to a simmer, and turn off the heat. Let stand 2 hours.

2. Preheat the oven to 325°F. Lightly grease two 8½ x 4½-inch loaf pans, line the bottoms with wax paper, and lightly grease the paper.

3. In a large mixing bowl, cream the butter and sugars together until light and fluffy, then gradually beat in the egg yolks, beating well after each addition. Add the vanilla and almond extracts and the orange rind and mix well.

4. In a separate bowl, stir together the flour, baking powder, salt, and spices until well blended. Gradually beat the flour mixture into the wet mixture, beating until well blended. Stir in the fruit and nut mixture with its liquid.

5. In a clean bowl and using clean beaters, whip the egg whites until stiff peaks form. Gently fold about 1 cup of the batter into the whites, then fold this mixture into the batter.

6. Transfer the batter to the prepared pans, place in the oven, and bake until the cakes are golden brown and a cake tester or wooden skewer inserted in the center comes out clean, about 1 hour. Transfer the pans to a wire rack and cool the cakes for 2 minutes or so, then remove the cakes from the pans, place on the rack, and cool completely.

7. Soak 2 rectangles of cheesecloth in the remaining brandy and wrap up the cakes with the cheesecloth, covering all surfaces. Wrap the wrapped cakes tightly in aluminum foil and store in a cool, dry place for 4 or 5 days before using.

Swedish Glögg

* * *

MAKES 3 WINE BOTTLES

This spicy mulled wine concoction is traditionally served warm on Christmas Eve after decorating the tree. I like to use it as a gift and I serve it in little cordial glasses as an after-dinner drink. Another (very untraditional) way to serve the glögg is as the base for a festive red-wine spritzer with a twist of orange.

> 2 bottles dry red wine
> 1/2 cup dried cranberries or golden raisins
> 1 cup sugar
> 1 teaspoon whole cloves
> 1 teaspoon cardamom seeds (optional)
> 2 cinnamon sticks, broken in half
> 2 1-inch knobs gingerroot, peeled and
>   crushed
> 1 orange rind, pith removed, and cut into strips
> 1 cup rum
> 1 cup brandy
> 1 1/2 cups vodka
> Blanched almonds

1. In a small, heavy saucepan, combine 2 cups of the red wine with the cranberries or raisins, sugar, spices, and orange rind. Place over medium-high heat and bring to a simmer.

2. Cover the pan, reduce the heat to low, and simmer very gently for 30 minutes. Remove from the heat and let stand 1 hour.

3. In a large bowl, preferably one with a spout, combine the remaining red wine, the rum, brandy, and vodka. Strain the spice mixture into the bowl. Pick out the cranberries and divide

them among 3 wine bottles. Pour the mixture through a funnel into the bottles and cork them.

4. Store the glögg in a cool place at least 2 days before using. Before giving the glögg, place a handful of blanched almonds in a cheesecloth bag and tie the bag to the neck of the bottle with a cord or ribbon. Include suggestions for serving, along with instructions that tradition calls for a few of the almonds to be placed in each glass.

NOTE The glögg can be gently rewarmed in a heavy, nonreactive pan over low heat. Do not allow to come to a boil.

The inexpensive new glass decanter is part of the gift.

Cookies!

Grandma Stapleton's
Bohemian Butter Cookies

Coconut Sugar Stars

Cinnamon Shortbread

Shortbread Scotties

Mocha Bars

Hazelnut Crescents

Gingerbread People

Vanilla Chip Cookies

Almond Matchsticks

Swedish Honey Cakes

Peanut Butter–Chocolate Chip Cookies

Peanut Butter and Jelly Thumbprints

When I was growing up, the first thing Mom and her mother, Grandma Wynn, did every year in preparation for Christmas was baking, baking, and more baking of cookies. The wonderful spicy smells that swept through the house was the "official" signal for the four of us kids that Christmas was just around the corner. We kids were put to work chopping nuts and other tasks, and Mom and Grandma baked hundreds of cookies, for our own use and for making up cookie trays for giving to our friends and neighbors. Year after year the cookies we kept for ourselves were packed into a big old lard tin that Mom kept in the cellar, and not even one could be tasted before Christmas Eve (all right, I'll admit that once or twice I may have snuck down to the cellar and snitched one!). So whenever I smell cookies baking, I'm a kid again and it's Christmas.

These are mostly very simple cookies like the ones Mom and Grandma made years ago (in fact, Mom baked all the cookies shown here), without any overly fussy decorations, but they're all very Christmasy just the same. Have fun!

These glass crocks of cutters and molds sit atop a cupboard in the kitchen all year long, but for the holidays I add big tartan bows. My young friends Michael and Stephen Stuzynski and Tiernan O'Rourke (opposite) sample the goods.

COOKIE BAKING TIPS
*

• Get the butter and eggs out of the refrigerator ahead of time so that they're at room temperature when you're ready to use them. Chop nuts and measure out other ingredients in the meantime.

• The dough for rolled cookies (such as Hazelnut Crescents, Gingerbread People, Grandma Stapleton's Bohemian Butter Cookies, and Coconut Sugar Stars) needs to be chilled to be firm enough before rolling out and cutting, so check the recipe and schedule the baking accordingly.

• If baking several kinds of cookies, schedule the cookies that need the same oven temperature to be baked one right after the other. This eliminates waiting for the oven to get hotter or cooler.

• For strongly flavored chocolate, spice, or peanut butter cookies, vegetable shortening can be substituted for butter, but for simple cookies I always use butter for its wonderful flavor.

• To finely chop or grind nuts, process in a food processor with quick on-and-off pulses. Do not overprocess or the nuts will become pasty.

• Cookies often get too brown on the bottom. To prevent this I use insulated baking sheets or regular baking sheets lined with baking parchment. Cookies will brown more evenly if baked on baking sheets without sides.

• If packed in tightly covered containers and stored in a cool but not cold place (an insulated but unheated porch, for example), cookies will keep well for 2 or 3 weeks. Cookies can be frozen for up to 2 months; to serve them at the spur of the moment, arrange cookies on a serving plate in a single layer and let them thaw for about 20 minutes—or thaw in the microwave.

Grandma Stapleton's Bohemian Butter Cookies

* * *

MAKES 3 TO 4 DOZEN
COOKIES, DEPENDING ON THE
SIZE OF THE CUTTERS

This recipe, brought to America by my great-grandmother, appeared in my first book, *The Holidays,* but I have to include it here, since Christmas just wouldn't be Christmas in my family without them. The coconut variation is a new idea.

> *2 cups (4 sticks) unsalted butter, softened*
> *1 cup sugar*
> *4 large eggs, 3 of them separated*
> *1 teaspoon vanilla extract*
> *4 cups unbleached all-purpose flour*
> *Assorted colored coarse sugars*

1. In a large mixing bowl, cream the butter and sugar together until light and smooth. Beat in the egg yolks, the remaining whole egg, and the vanilla. Reserve the egg whites.

2. One cup at a time, beat the flour into the wet mixture to form a soft dough. Form the dough into a ball, wrap tightly, and refrigerate 3 hours.

3. Preheat the oven to 350°F. Lightly grease baking sheets.

4. On a lightly floured surface, roll out the dough to a thickness of ⅛ inch. Cut out shapes

For the kids, we made cookie trees (above left) by cutting out Coconut Sugar Stars in six sizes, stacking them, then topping them with red gumdrops. The pineapple-shaped cookies (left, decorated with gold dragées) express the traditional symbol of welcome.

with floured cookie cutters, then transfer the cookies to the prepared baking sheets.

5. Lightly beat the egg whites. Using a pastry brush, glaze the surfaces of the cookies by brushing with the egg whites. Decorate each cookie with a sprinkling of colored sugar.

6. Bake until the edges of the cookies are lightly browned, 8 to 10 minutes, then remove to wire racks to cool. Store the cookies in tightly covered containers for up to 2 months in a cool place or freeze up to 6 months.

Coconut Sugar Stars Add 1¼ cups shredded coconut at the end of step 2. Use star-shaped cutters to cut out the cookies, and decorate them with colored sugar.

Cinnamon Shortbread

* * *

MAKES 2 DOZEN COOKIES

1 cup (2 sticks) unsalted butter, softened
½ cup confectioners' sugar
1 teaspoon vanilla extract
2 cups unbleached all-purpose flour
2 tablespoons ground cinnamon
¼ teaspoon salt
Confectioners' sugar, for dusting

1. Preheat the oven to 300°F.

2. In a mixing bowl, cream the butter and sugar together until light and fluffy, then beat in the vanilla. In a separate bowl, sift together the flour, cinnamon, and salt. Beat the dry mixture into the wet mixture to form a soft dough.

3. Divide the dough in half, then roll each half

into 2 circles about 8 inches in diameter and place the dough circles on a large greased baking sheet. (Or press the dough into 2 greased 8-inch round cake pans.) Using a sharp knife, score the dough about halfway through into 12 wedges. Using a table fork, crimp the outer edge of the circle, then prick a pattern into the surface of each wedge.

4. Bake until the edges are very lightly brown, 35 to 40 minutes. Cool about 5 minutes, then cut into wedges and cool completely. Dust the shortbread lightly with confectioners' sugar. Pack into wax paper-lined tins, cover tightly, and store in a cool place for up to 3 months.

Shortbread Scotties Roll out the dough, use a Scottie-shaped cutter to make cutout cookies, and bake on ungreased baking sheets. These will bake a little more quickly than the circles.

Bake Cinnamon Shortbread in the traditional wedge shape or use Scottie-shaped cutters to cut them out.

Mocha Bars
* * *

MAKES 52 BAR COOKIES

¾ cup vegetable shortening, melted
1½ cups granulated sugar
¾ cup unsweetened cocoa
1 tablespoon instant espresso powder (not
    granules)
3 large eggs, lightly beaten
1 teaspoon vanilla extract
¾ cup unbleached all-purpose flour
½ teaspoon salt
½ cup finely chopped hazelnuts or
    pecans, lightly toasted

Glaze
1 tablespoon unsalted butter, melted
2 tablespoons milk
1 tablespoon unsweetened cocoa
½ cup confectioners' sugar
½ teaspoon vanilla extract

1. Preheat the oven to 350°F. Lightly grease a 9 x 13-inch baking pan.

2. In a mixing bowl, combine the shortening, sugar, cocoa, and espresso powder and beat until smooth, then beat in the eggs and vanilla. Beat in the flour and salt, then stir in the nuts.

3. Transfer the batter to the prepared pan and bake until the edges are just beginning to pull away from the pan and a cake tester or wooden skewer inserted in the center comes out clean, 35 to 40 minutes. Remove the pan to a wire rack and allow the cake to cool.

4. To make the glaze, combine all the ingredi-

ents in a small bowl and beat with a fork until smooth. Drizzle the glaze in a circular pattern over the cake. When the glaze is firm, cut the cake into 1 x 2¼-inch bars.

5. Pack the bars in a tightly covered container in individual layers with wax paper between each layer. Store in a cool place up to 1 week. (To keep the bars from hardening, place a slice of apple, loosely wrapped in wax paper, in with the cookies.)

Hazelnut Crescents
* * *

MAKES ABOUT 5 DOZEN COOKIES

2 3-ounce packages cream cheese, softened
1 cup (2 sticks) unsalted butter
1 cup granulated sugar
½ teaspoon salt
2 cups unbleached all-purpose flour

Filling
½ cup ground hazelnuts
½ cup firmly packed light brown sugar
1 teaspoon ground cinnamon

Confectioners' sugar, for dusting

1. In a mixing bowl, combine the cream cheese, butter, sugar, salt, and flour and beat until blended, forming a dough. Form the dough into a ball, wrap well, and chill for 3 hours.

2. Preheat the oven to 375°F. In a small bowl, combine the filling ingredients and mix. Set aside.

3. On a lightly floured surface, roll out the dough to a thickness of about ⅛ inch. Sprinkle the filling mixture evenly over the dough and lightly press it into the surface of the dough. Cut

An assortment of holiday cookies—from Old World elegant Hazelnut Crescents (above) to homey Mocha Bars (above right) and old-fashioned Vanilla Chips (right).

the dough into 3-inch squares, then cut each square in half diagonally.

4. Roll up each triangle, beginning with the longest side and leaving the pointed corner on the outside. Place about an inch apart, point side down, on ungreased baking sheets and curve each roll slightly to form a crescent. Bake until golden brown, 5 to 7 minutes.

5. Remove the cookies to a wire rack to cool for 5 minutes, dust lightly with confectioners' sugar, and cool completely. Pack the cookies in tightly covered containers and store in a cool place.

Gingerbread People

* * *

MAKES 2 TO 3 DOZEN
COOKIES, DEPENDING ON THE
SIZE OF THE CUTTERS

Aside from the more obvious purpose of eating these cookies, I like making them to hang on my little kitchen tree. To make the cookies easy to hang, poke a hole into the top of each cookie with a wooden skewer just before baking. After the cookies are baked and cooled, carefully poke the skewer through the holes, then poke cord or skinny ribbons through the holes and tie into loops for hanging.

1 cup (2 sticks) unsalted butter, softened
1 cup firmly packed light brown sugar
¾ cup dark molasses
1 large egg, lightly beaten
5 cups unbleached all-purpose flour
1 teaspoon salt
1½ teaspoons baking powder
2 teaspoons ground ginger
2 teaspoons ground cinnamon
1½ teaspoons ground cloves
½ teaspoon grated nutmeg

Dried currants, for decorating

1. In a large mixing bowl, cream the butter, sugar, and molasses until smooth, then beat in the egg. In a separate bowl, sift together the flour, salt, baking powder, and spices, then beat the dry mixture into the wet mixture until well blended. Shape the dough into a ball, wrap it tightly, and chill until firm, about 3 hours.

2. Preheat the oven to 350°F. Lightly grease baking sheets. Divide the dough into 2 parts and return one half to the refrigerator. On a lightly floured work surface (or between 2 sheets of wax paper), roll out the other half to a thickness of about ⅛ inch. Cut out the cookies and, using a spatula, transfer them to the baking sheets.

3. Lightly press currants into the dough to make eyes and buttons. Bake until the edges of the cookies are nicely browned, 10 to 12 minutes, then remove the cookies to wire racks to cool. Roll out and bake the remaining dough.

4. When the cookies are cool, pack them in individual layers, with wax paper between the layers, in tightly covered containers and store in a cool place.

Vanilla Chip Cookies

* * *

MAKES ABOUT 4 DOZEN COOKIES

Believe it or not, there are some people near and dear to me who are not particularly fond of chocolate. These cookies, with lots of vanilla flavor (the recipe calls for 1 *table*spoon of vanilla extract in addition to the chips), are for them.

1 cup (2 sticks) unsalted butter, softened
1 cup firmly packed light brown sugar
1 cup granulated sugar
2 large eggs
1 tablespoon vanilla extract
2 cups unbleached all-purpose flour
1 teaspoon baking powder
½ teaspoon salt

½ teaspoon ground cinnamon
1 cup chopped walnuts
1¼ cups vanilla chips (white baking chips)

1. Preheat the oven to 375°F. Lightly grease baking sheets.

2. In a mixing bowl, cream the butter and sugars together until smooth, then beat in the eggs and vanilla. In a separate bowl, sift together the flour, baking powder, salt, and cinnamon. Gradually beat the dry mixture into the wet mixture, then stir in the nuts and chips.

3. Drop the dough by spoonfuls about 2 inches apart onto the prepared baking sheets. Bake until the cookies are nicely browned, 10 to 12 minutes. Transfer the cookies to wire racks to cool, then store in tightly covered containers.

Almond Matchsticks
* * *

MAKES ABOUT 5 DOZEN COOKIES

When my friend Carmela Moeller, who owns the Buchmeister bookstore here in Chatham with her husband, Hal, brought these to my house, I had no idea that they were one of my own recipes in disguise. Carmela softened the dough of the Sugar-Almond Christmas Cookies in *Simple Pleasures* by adding cream cheese, shaped the cookies differently by using a cookie press, and dipped the ends of the baked cookies in melted chocolate, giving them their characteristic "matchstick" appearance.

Chop the nuts by pulsing them in a food processor until they're fine but not pasty.

½ cup (1 stick) unsalted butter, softened
1 3-ounce package cream cheese, softened
¾ cup sugar
1 large egg
4 teaspoons milk
1 teaspoon almond extract
1 teaspoon vanilla extract
1¼ cups unbleached all-purpose flour
¼ teaspoon baking powder
¼ teaspoon salt
¾ cup very finely chopped almonds
2 to 3 ounces semisweet chocolate, melted

1. Preheat the oven to 375°F. Lightly grease baking sheets.

2. In a large mixing bowl, cream together the butter, cream cheese, and sugar. Beat in the egg and milk, then beat in the almond extract and the vanilla. In a separate bowl combine the flour, baking powder, and salt, then gradually add the dry mixture to the wet mixture, mixing well after each addition. Add the almonds and mix well.

3. In batches, transfer the dough to a cookie press or pastry tube fitted with a medium star tip (about ⅜ inch). Pipe 2½-inch strips of dough onto the baking sheets, about 2 inches apart.

4. Bake the cookies until the edges are lightly browned, 8 to 10 minutes, then remove the cookies to wire racks to cool. One at a time, dip the end of each cookie into the melted chocolate to cover about ⅜ inch of the cookie with the chocolate. Place the cookies back onto the racks to allow the chocolate to harden.

5. Pack the cookies in tightly covered containers with wax paper between the layers and store in a cool place.

Almond Matchsticks on a paper doily-lined plate and Swedish Honey Cakes served on a ruby Depression glass plate.

Swedish Honey Cakes

* * *

MAKES ABOUT 8 DOZEN
COOKIES

*T*hese almond-topped cookies are flavored with lemon and spice, a classic Scandinavian combination. They're the perfect accompaniment to a cup of hot tea.

1 cup honey
Juice and grated rind of 1 lemon
2¾ cups unbleached all-purpose flour
2 cups confectioners' sugar
1½ teaspoons baking soda
½ teaspoon salt
1 tablespoon ground cinnamon
1 tablespoon ground ginger
1 teaspoon ground cloves
3 large eggs, lightly beaten
1 teaspoon almond extract

½ cup finely chopped blanched almonds
½ cup finely chopped candied lemon peel
1 cup sliced almonds, approximately

1. Preheat the oven to 350°F. Lightly grease baking sheets.

2. Combine the honey and lemon juice in a small saucepan and stir to mix well. Place over medium heat and bring to a boil. Remove from the heat and allow to cool to lukewarm.

3. In a mixing bowl, sift together the flour, confectioners' sugar, baking soda, salt, and spices, then beat in the honey mixture, eggs, and almond extract. Stir in the chopped almonds, candied lemon peel, and grated lemon rind.

4. Cover the bowl tightly and chill the dough overnight.

5. Drop the dough by scant teaspoonfuls onto the prepared baking sheets and cover each dough drop with sliced almonds. Bake until the cookies are nicely browned, 8 to 10 minutes. Carefully transfer the cookies (the cookies will be quite soft) to wire racks to cool, then pack in tightly covered containers and store in a cool place.

Peanut Butter–Chocolate Chip Cookies

✳ ✳ ✳

MAKES ABOUT 5 DOZEN
COOKIES

½ cup (1 stick) unsalted butter, softened,
    or *vegetable shortening*
1 cup smooth peanut butter
½ cup firmly packed light brown sugar
½ cup granulated sugar
2 large eggs, lightly beaten
1 teaspoon vanilla extract
1½ cups unbleached all-purpose flour
½ teaspoon baking soda
¼ teaspoon baking powder
¼ teaspoon salt
½ cup semisweet miniature chocolate chips

1. Preheat the oven to 375°F. Lightly grease baking sheets.

2. In a mixing bowl, cream the butter, peanut butter, and sugars together until smooth, then beat in the eggs and vanilla. In a separate bowl, sift together the flour, baking soda, baking powder, and salt.

3. Beat the dry mixture into the wet mixture until just blended, then stir in the chocolate chips.

4. Drop rounded tablespoons of dough onto ungreased baking sheets, then flatten slightly with a fork, making a stripe pattern in the dough.

5. Bake until the edges are nicely browned, about 8 minutes. Leave the cookies on the baking sheets for a minute or two, then transfer them to wire racks to cool.

Peanut Butter and Jelly Thumbprints Omit the chocolate chips from the dough. Shape the dough into ¾-inch balls. Place the balls about 2 inches apart on baking sheets and flatten them slightly with the bottom of a glass. Make an impression in each ball with the tip of a pinkie and fill each impression with a little dab of strawberry or apricot jam, then bake as above. Makes about 8 dozen.

I like to serve old-fashioned peanut butter cookies from old-fashioned plates like this green Depression glass one.

Wreaths, Bouquets, and Other Greenery

Making wreaths and bouquets and draping everything around the house that will hold still long enough with greenery has been one of my favorite parts of holiday preparations since I was little. My aunt Florence, Dad's sister, was my Christmastime mentor. She was known all across her area in Ohio for her wonderful holiday decorations inside and out, and she even won a few local awards for them. Her motto was "At Christmastime, you can *never* overdo it," a motto I learned early on to adopt for myself.

Every year Aunt Florence would take me along the back roads and woods to gather beautiful things from winter nature, such as white birch branches, greens, evergreen cones, dried weeds, grapevines, and winter berries. Even though Aunt Florence is long gone, this tradition is one I still carry out every year. When I'm out on the back roads here in New Jersey on my way home with the car loaded down with nature, I laugh to myself as I hear Aunt Florence's voice: "You can *never* overdo it."

The pinecone and nut wreath (left) was made by wiring clumps of 2 or 3 pinecones together, then wiring the clumps onto a store-bought straw wreath base, covering it completely. The nuts were attached with Elmer's glue.

Sometimes, the simpler the better (opposite, top). This rustic wreath, hanging from a rafter, is nothing more than grapevines and bittersweet vines tied up with brown twine. An old railroad lantern hangs from the same nail.

The ribbon wreath (opposite, bottom) was made by wiring lots of bows onto a store-bought boxwood wreath.

My neighbors Alison and Warren Eversfield are natives of New Zealand, and when they came to America they brought the charming holiday tradition of this good luck candy wreath (above) with them. When visitors go out the door on their way home, they each snip one candy from the wreath as a wish for good luck from the hosts.

To make the wreath every year, Warren starts by wrapping an embroidery hoop with crumpled aluminum foil. He uses strong cotton thread to attach foil-wrapped candies, crowding them together as closely as possible. A small pair of scissors is hung from the wreath with a ribbon to make the candies easy to snip off.

27

Basic Wreath Making

* * *

I often start out with unadorned wreaths bought at a nursery or florist, since so many varieties are available nowadays, but sometimes I'll make my own from scratch. Either a straw or grapevine wreath can be used as a base; a straw wreath will yield a bulkier result. Any combination of greenery (evergreens, such as boxwood, spruce, juniper, or cedar; magnolia or lemon leaves; bunches of dried herbs; and so on) can be used in making the wreath, but I pre-

fer to make the basic wreath all the same and to use the other materials as decoration. Having an extra pair of hands available to help hold things down as they're wired on is a big help.

Materials
A straw or grapevine wreath, any size
Greenery boughs and sprigs
*Florist's wire (gauge depends on the
    thickness and weight of the greenery)*
*Additional greenery and other adornments
    (such as berries, dried fruits,
    pinecones, ribbons—you name it)*
Florist's picks

28

1. Secure the first bough at the stem end with the end of the wire (do not cut the wire). Add an additional bough, overlapping the bud ends to cover the previous stem, and secure it by continuing to uncoil the wire and wrapping it around the stem end of each bough and the wreath. Continue this process until the base wreath is covered, front and sides.

2. Make a wire loop from which to hang the wreath and secure it to the wreath (this is much easier to do before adding the other decorations). Using twists of wire or florist's picks, secure the other decorations to the wreath.

This pretty little wreath (opposite) began with a bought grapevine wreath, then many small sprigs of pepperberries were wired on. Wired ribbon was wrapped around the wreath, then it was finished off with fresh-cut sprigs of boxwood tucked into the ribbons.

The wreath above left, decorated in a traditional southern style, began with an unadorned magnolia leaf wreath bought at my local nursery. To decorate it, I began by wiring on small branches of pyracantha (firethorn). To attach the clementines, lady apples, and limes I skewered them, then pushed wires through the holes.

A wreath for the kitchen (above) is a store-bought one— I added store-bought dried pomegranates, dried orange and apple slices (pages 44–45), and cinnamon sticks.

KEEPING GREENERY FRESH

*

• No greens that are store-bought will ever be as fresh as greens you cut yourself. Take a good look at what's available around in your garden, those of your neighbors and friends (ask before clipping!), and the wild.

• As soon as greens, store-bought or otherwise, are brought home, they should be placed in a bucket of water and left in a cool place overnight so they absorb as much water as possible. (Trim an inch or so from the stem ends of bought greens first to have a fresher cut.) Before use, dry the stem ends well, then dip them in a little melted paraffin to seal in the moisture.

• Lightly mist wreaths and other arrangements daily with plain water, being careful not to mist everything in the house.

This year I hung a basket on the front door (left) instead of a wreath. It was filled with blue spruce, juniper, holly, and dried red coxcombs. Apples and pinecones were wired in, and it was all finished off with twigs of curly willow. Many other combinations could be used as well, bearing in mind that dried flowers should only be used when a porch protects the bouquet from the weather and especially fragile ones are best left indoors.

Every year I do something a little bit different with the garlands that wrap the posts on my front porch (above), but I always start with old-fashioned white pine roping intertwined with strings of lights. Then I tuck in sprigs of blue spruce, juniper, and holly. This year I added some magnolia leaves and wired on shiny red apples, pinecones, and artichokes. Finally, twigs of curly willow, gathered from the wild, are tucked into the greenery.

THE FLORAL TOOLKIT
*

None of the ideas in this book requires items that are particularly expensive or hard to find, but many of the projects will go much more smoothly if you have a well-equipped toolbox. Here's a list of the things I keep on hand, not only during the holiday season but for use all year long. Most of these items are available from floral supply houses, the local florist, or craft shops.

Wired wooden floral picks, in several lengths

22- or 24-gauge florist's wire

Hot glue gun and glue sticks

Elmer's glue

Chunks of florist's oasis

Florist's tape

Brown twine

Florist's clay (good for securing candles in candleholders, too)

Coated metal or glass frogs, for use in containers

Small garden clippers

Chicken wire

Any number of simple "bouquets" can be created in a matter of only a few minutes, and without having to form a search party for the makings. Here are a few easy ideas that I particularly like.

Small branches of bittersweet and a few sprigs of holly (above, left) were casually tossed onto this big, shallow cobalt glass bowl, making a festive combination of colors

A trug (above) is filled with clove-studded oranges, limes, clementines, and evergreens, with a gold ribbon.

I filled this big basket (below) with an assortment of greens from out back, dried leaves, twigs of curly willow and hawthorn, and foot-long cinnamon sticks.

Collections

I'll admit to being an insatiable collecter and the number of my collections is probably higher than I'm willing to admit, but I do get a certain amount of pleasure from moving my collections around the house and replacing one with another for a while. This year I had to admit to myself that my Santa collection won't fit on the mantel any longer, even if I divide the collection into cat-egories and put only one category up. And I also had to admit that I have a few more holiday collections than I'd realized. And then there are the collections that are out all year round and really have nothing to do with Christmas but seem to take on a Christmasy aspect during the holiday season. Here are some of my collections, along with those of a few of my friends.

Mantels are the perfect place for holiday displays. Here are collections of birdhouses with old-fashioned "toy" trees (opposite), cobalt glass vases and pitchers with white-wired lights (above), and teddies draped with wooden cranberry beads (below).

A collection of Santa pillows old and new (opposite) dresses up the bed in the guest bedroom.

Every year I get a kick out of unpacking my odd assortment of vintage holiday table linens (opposite, below).

I didn't consciously begin collecting little snowmen, but here they are (right), gathered together on a small table in the kitchen.

This year I gathered together as many of my Santas as I could possibly fit together on one table.

Trees of Every Shape and Size

There are moments that happen annually that are important to me at Christmastime and I *must* feel them every year: a trip to see Macy's in New York, the tree at Rockefeller Center, and the Fifth Avenue windows at Lord & Taylor. Or a nighttime trip in the car to see everyone's lights. But one of the moments that seems the most wonderful is the opening of the boxes and unpacking of the Christmas tree ornaments, with sighs of "remember this one?" and "oh, look, here's the little . . . "

The trees that I've seen and liked best have always been those that are decorated with a somewhat haphazard eye and a sense of humor, the trees that reflect their owner's experiences and personalities. For instance, when my friends Jonni and Joe Ryder lived in France for a year, they had no Christmas ornaments, so they decorated their little tabletop tree with lights, ribbons, and the caps from Champagne bottles that were opened during the holiday season.

When there's a traditional tree in the house I don't mind trees with themes, but I really don't care much for overly "designed" trees at home— those are best left to the tree-trimming sections of department stores. Here are a few ideas for "main event" trees as well as a few decorative ones for other parts of the house.

No matter what any of the trendy style setters say, to me, there's no tree more Christmasy than one decorated with lots of brightly colored and shining molded glass ornaments. I've been collecting these ornaments for as long as I can remember, and my collection now ranges from a large, heavy glass ball that belonged to my great-grandparents to a 1950s ball inscribed with SILENT NIGHT, to a brand-new reproduction of a Victorian Santa Claus.

To decorate my tree, I start with a combination of old-fashioned colored lights for warmth and tiny white lights for sparkle. Next the tree is draped with different-colored strings of glass beads that have been wound together. Next, we always tuck solid-colored glass ornaments into the depths of the tree to reflect the lights; we use the more decorative ornaments toward the ends of the branches. The last decorations to go on are hundreds of glass icicles at the tips of the branches, turning the tree into a magical thing.

Toothpick trees from the sixties are due for a revival.

I made the ornaments below years ago using plain five-and-dime "satin" Christmas balls, all kinds of "pearls" and beads, straight pins and hat pins, paper and dressmaker's trimmings, and assorted ribbons.

Toothpick Trees

* * *

When we were kids one of our favorite pre-Christmas pastimes was making toothpick trees, which seems to be almost forgotten these days. When I decided to renew the custom last year, I couldn't remember exactly how we did it and neither did Mom or my brothers or sister. Well, my old friend Nolan Drummond, a fellow Ohioan, remembers, and here they are. Years ago we used to decorate the trees with tiny colored glass balls, but now I like them just as they are.

This is a great group project for adults and children alike; one evening, four of us made three trees in a few hours while we sipped mulled cider.

Materials
6 to 10 boxes round toothpicks
12 to 20 2-inch Styrofoam balls
1 8- or 9-inch Styrofoam disk
Several sheets of newspaper
Large cardboard box
Flat white spray paint
Spray snow

1. Poke toothpicks about ½ inch into the Styrofoam balls, placing the picks very close together and covering the balls completely. One box of 250 toothpicks will cover about 2 balls.

2. Arrange several balls in a circle on the Styrofoam disk and gently push them together so the toothpick balls stay together and they stick to the disk. Using 1 or 2 fewer balls, arrange a second circle atop the first one, and gently push it down to make it adhere. Continue until the tree is the size and width you want.

3. In a well-ventilated work area, spread out several sheets of newspaper, then place a large cardboard box on its side on the paper. Place the tree inside the box and spray it lightly on all sides with the white paint. Allow to dry.

4. Spray the tree lightly with the spray snow, then allow it to dry. Continue adding light coats of snow until the tree is as fluffy as you'd like (we used 3 coats for our trees).

NOTE The trees are fragile, so they should be wrapped in tissue and carefully packed in a strong box for storage. Rejuvenate the trees each year with a light spray of snow if necessary.

Way back in June, Nolan Drummond and Ken Daniels discovered this magnificent tree in the woods behind their Connecticut house. Decorated with scores of snowflakes crocheted by Nolan, along with a smattering of other ornaments collected over the years, the mighty evergreen occupies half of the large, cathedral-ceilinged living room.

SELECTING A CUT TREE
✳

• Inspect the needles. They should be flexible and not brittle and should not pull off easily (a few will fall off of even the freshest tree).

• The branches should be flexible but firm.

• Look for a trunk that is sticky with sap.

I always have a little tree in the kitchen (far left), decorated with colorful old-fashioned bubble lights (yes, they're still being made!) and little white lights, Gingerbread People (page 22), strings of gumdrops, little pinecones, and some of my favorite cookie cutters.

Simple shapes were cut out of construction paper (left), strung with twine, and hung on a twig tree along with strings of cranberries and popcorn.

Larry Terricone decorated this tree (far left, below) with a collection of stuffed teddy bears.

The grapevine tree (left, below) was decorated with tiny yellow and white lights, a variety of dried flowers, little bird's nests, and artificialbirds.

This idea (right) came about a few years ago, when I was moving right after the holidays. I didn't want to get all the boxes of regular ornaments out of storage, so I decorated my tree with reproductions of Victorian "scrap" Santas, crocheted snowflakes, glass icicles, and ribbon bows, all of which fit flat into one shopping bag when Christmas was over, ready to move.

Lights and Scents of Christmas

Christmastime Potpourri

Citrus Pomanders

Dried Orange Slices

Dried Apple Rings

"Luminaries"

Wrapped Votive Candleholders

A Few Homemade Candles

We all have vivid recollections of the sights and sounds of Christmases past that instantly evoke the holiday spirit. And it seems awfully difficult to imagine Christmas without all the wonderful aromas we associate with the season—pine, cedar, citrus, apple, and spice—wafting their way all over the house. It just wouldn't be Christmas at all.

The same goes for candles and lights. I set out candles of all shapes, colors, and sizes every-where. And even if late December is unseasonably warm, I keep a fire going in the fireplace, with a window or two open, if need be, so I can smell the wood burning, listen to its crackle, and feel the glow.

Here are a few easy ideas for making the house smell good when you walk in the door and for making it glow.

Christmastime Potpourri
* * *

Here's a basic potpourri recipe that can be fiddled with endlessly, depending on the availability of the ingredients and individual tastes. Select the ingredients for both color and aroma, and make sure that all the ingredients are well dried. The only essential is the orris root, available at herbal or floral supply shops or craft shops, which helps preserve the scents of the ingredients. A few drops of a compatible essential oil can be added when making the potpourri or later on to refresh its aroma.

Materials

Dried rose petals and/or small rosebuds
Dried lavender
Fragrant evergreen needles
Strips of citrus rind (lemon, lime, orange,
  tangerine), cut from the fruit with a
  vegetable peeler and dried on a rack
Bay leaves
Sprigs of rosemary
Eucalyptus leaves (these are pungent,
  so use sparingly)
Holly leaves and berries
Cinnamon sticks
Dried Orange Slices (page 44), Dried
  Apple Rings (page 45)
Whole allspice and cloves
Little evergreen cones
Cedar shavings
1 teaspoon powdered dried orris root for
  every 4 cups of other ingredients
A few drops essential oil (balsam, rose,
  lavender, cinnamon, vanilla, and so on)

1. In a large bowl, combine the selected petals, leaves, and spices and toss lightly with a wooden spoon. Sprinkle the orris root and oil over all and toss again.

2. Pack the potpourri loosely in large jars or other nonmetallic containers and cover the containers with brown paper (cut-up grocery bags work well) secured with rubber bands or twine. Store in a cool, dark place for a week or so to allow the scents to mingle and mellow. Gently stir the potpourri every few days.

For gift-giving we packaged our potpourri in new terra-cotta plant saucers, but pretty old saucers or small bowls picked up at tag sales would be nice as well.

GIFT-PACKAGING POTPOURRI
❋

• Pack the potpourri loosely into small cellophane bags (available at floral supply or craft shops). Tie the bags up by using kitchen string or twist ties, and cover the string with ribbons.

• Use little muslin bags to make potpourri sachets, tie them up with ribbons, and package a few sachets together in a small tin.

• Fill terra-cotta saucers with the mixture, then wrap them up with cellophane. Ribbon, cord, or raffia finishes off the package. The recipient can simply unwrap the saucer and set it right out.

Citrus Pomanders

* * *

A spice-covered pomander hanging in a doorway or from a doorknob or bedpost brings a nice aroma into a room or a closet. They're wonderful gifts as well. Make these early in December so they're ready for the holidays.

Materials

¼ cup ground cinnamon
2 tablespoons ground cloves
1 tablespoon ground allspice
1 tablespoon grated nutmeg
1 tablespoon powdered dried orris root
6 oranges, lemons, and/or tangerines
A long thin nail or skewer
Whole cloves
Ribbon
Straight pins

1. In a small bowl, combine the ground cinnamon, cloves, allspice, and grated nutmeg with the orris root and mix well. Leaving a ½-inch-wide strip around the circumference of the fruit, pierce the fruit rind, making holes about ¼ inch apart in straight rows (or create another decorative pattern, perhaps spirals or concentric circles). Press a clove into each hole.

2. Place a few tablespoonfuls of the spice mixture in the bottom of a bowl large enough to hold all the fruit. One at a time, place a clove-studded fruit in the bowl and sprinkle with additional spice mixture, then sprinkle all the fruit with the remaining mixture.

3. Turn the fruit daily, rotating the fruits from top to bottom, then spooning the spice mixture over all. Continue this curing process until the fruits harden, 2 to 3 weeks.

4. Wrap a ½-inch-wide ribbon around each pomander, secure it with straight pins, and tie the ribbon into a bow.

Dried Orange Slices

* * *

T hese are nice for making garlands, decorating wreaths, and tying onto presents.

Materials

Ground cinnamon
Sugar
Oranges

1. Preheat the oven to 200°F. Place a wire rack on a baking sheet.

2. In a shallow bowl, combine the cinnamon and sugar—1 teaspoon ground cinnamon to each ½ cup of sugar.

3. Horizontally cut the oranges into ⅛-inch-thick slices. One at a time, dip the oranges into the cinnamon-sugar mixture, coating them lightly on both sides. Arrange the orange slices in a single layer on the rack.

4. Place in the oven and bake until the oranges are dried and lightly glazed, 2 to 3 hours (timing will depend on the juiciness of the oranges and on the oven temperature).

5. Remove the pan from the oven and let the oranges stand on the rack overnight. Pack the slices in loosely covered containers, with absorbent paper between the layers, until using.

Dried Apple Rings
* * *

*M*ake garlands of these fragrant dried apple rings strung on brown twine with bay leaves and cinnamon sticks, or use them as part of the decoration on wreaths. Note that these apple rings are for decoration only, not for eating. Red Delicious apples, with their bright red skins that darken beautifully when the fruit is dried, are ideal for making apple rings.

Materials
1½ parts ground cinnamon
½ part ground cloves
1 part powdered dried orris root
Apples

1. In a small shallow bowl (a soup plate is ideal), stir together the cinnamon, cloves, and orris root. Set aside.

2. Preheat the oven to 200°F.

3. Using an apple corer or a small, sharp knife, remove a small cylinder from the center of each apple, then slice the apples horizontally into ¼-inch slices.

4. One at a time, roll the apple slices in the spice mixture, coating them well. Place the apple rings on a baking sheet in a single layer. Place the pan in the oven until the apple rings are well dried, 2 to 3 hours.

5. Place the baking sheet on a wire rack and allow the apple rings to cool to room temperature. If the rings are not to be used right away, pack them in a loosely covered container in a cool place.

"INSTANT" CHRISTMAS
*

With a couple of candles already glowing, nothing else makes a room more Christmasy than the wonderful aromas we all associate with the holidays. When the holiday baking is being done, the house already smells of Christmas, but here are a few other ways to quickly spread Christmas all over.

• Pile pinecones into a basket or pretty bowl and dot them with a few drops of balsam or spicy essential oils.

• Dab fragrant essential oil onto unlit lightbulbs. When the lights are turned on, their low heat will spread the fragrance.

• Even if you don't have a tree, a few boughs of fragrant evergreens over a doorway will help give a Christmasy aroma.

• Toss strips of orange and/or lemon rind into a pot (or use a whole fruit, thinly sliced) with some whole cloves, whole allspice, a bay leaf, and a cinnamon stick or two. Cover with water and let the mixture simmer gently, uncovered, to perfume the house. Add more water as necessary.

• After peeling citrus fruit, place the strips of peel in a small pretty bowl along with a broken cinnamon stick and a few cloves. Toss daily.

• Hang fragrant Gingerbread People (page 22) from a small tree in the kitchen.

• When building a fire for the fireplace, add a few cinnamon sticks or a few fresh evergreen branches.

• Use naturally scented candles—bayberry, balsam, vanilla, or spice.

• Don't forget the upstairs—scent bathrooms, bedrooms, and guest rooms, too.

"Luminaries"
✳ ✳ ✳

The first year I lived in Chatham, a group gathered for supper on Christmas Eve at my house. Shortly after my first guests left, the phone rang. "Get in the car and come for a ride downtown! Don't ask why, just do it!" was the message. So the rest of us piled into the car and off we went, soon to be greeted by the most magical sight. All along the roads and walkways, hundreds and hundreds of glowing paper lanterns lit the way. This heartwarming custom originated in the Southwest, and the real name for the glowing bags is *farolitos*—"little lanterns"—but here in the Northeast, everyone calls them luminaries.

Materials
White paper bags, about 12 inches high
Sand or Kitty Litter
Votive candles

1. Fold down the top 2 inches or so of each bag, making a stiffening "collar." Scoop about 2 cups of sand into each bag.

2. Place the bags along the road and/or walkway (or atop a stone or brick wall) 6 to 12 feet apart, making sure the bags are on a flat, even surface. Place a candle into each bag, pushing it down into the sand to anchor it.

3. Use long matches or a butane fire starter to light the candles.

For extra shimmer, this year I added clusters of colored lights (above, left) to my window wreaths and porch posts. Luminaries line the front walk on Christmas Eve.

My big light-up Santas are gathered by the gazebo (left), a view I enjoy whenever I sit at the kitchen window.

46

Groupings of lights always look more spectacular than just one or two. On the sideboard (above, left), I gathered glass and silver candlesticks on a round mirror and added tiny Christmas lights and silvery balls.

A collection of old and new oil lamps (left) are gathered together on a table in the hall and decorated with bows.

Plain glass votive candleholders (above) have been decorated with bay leaves, cinnamon sticks, and even peppermint sticks. To make the holders, attach the decorations with double-sided tape or tiny balls of florist's clay (if using leaves, overlap them slightly to cover the tape or clay). Carefully tie narrow ribbons around the holders to secure the decorations.

In the background (above), little terra-cotta flowerpots, decorated with sprigs of evergreen and berries, also serve as holders for little votive candles.

Basic Candle Making
* * *

$\mathcal{M}$aking your own candles is rewarding, especially after looking at the prices of some of the fancier candles in the shops. And it's always fun to unmold the candles, finding that it really worked!

Basic Materials
Equal amounts of paraffin and beeswax
Candlewicks (B-1 for smaller candles, B-2
  for larger ones)
Wooden skewers
Candle coloring sticks or colored crayons
Essential fragrance oils (for scenting the
  candles)
Molds, such as milk cartons, plastic pint
  and quart containers

For Decorative Candles
Bay leaves or dried sage leaves
Evergreen sprigs
Sprigs of bitterberries
Ice cubes

1. In a small, heavy saucepan over low heat, melt the wax, stir in the coloring and/or scent, then remove the pan from the heat. Cut the wicks, making them about 2 inches longer than the height of the molds. Dip the wicks into the melted wax, then lay them on a wire rack to dry and harden.

2. Tie one end of each wick around a wooden skewer, then lay the skewer across the top of the mold with the wick centered straight down.

3. In a heavy, medium pan over low heat, melt equal amounts of paraffin and beeswax. If the candles are to be colored, tint the wax with candle color or crayons. Remove the pan from the heat. If the candles are to be scented, stir in about ½ teaspoon essential fragrance oil per cup of wax. Allow the wax to cool slightly.

4. Carefully pour the wax into the mold, leaving about ½-inch space at the top. Allow the wax to cool completely. To unmold, dip the mold into a pan of hot water to loosen the candle.

"Swiss Cheese" Candles That's what we called them when I was growing up because of their hole-filled texture. To make them, first cut the tops from milk cartons or other wax-coated paper containers. Place a waxed wick in the center of a carton, then fill the carton loosely with ice cubes. Pour warm wax into the carton and allow it to cool and the ice to melt. Over a sink or large bowl, rip the carton off the candles and allow all the water to drip out. Dry the candles thoroughly before packing or using.

Naturally Decorated Candles Place one mold of similar shape (I use half-gallon and quart-sized ice cream and yogurt cartons) inside another and place sprigs of cedar, sage, or whole bay leaves in between the 2 molds. Fill the inner mold with ice and carefully fill the outer mold with hot wax, trying to keep the decorations pressed against the sides of the outer mold. Allow the ice to melt and the wax to cool, then pour out the water and remove the inner mold completely. Place a wick over the hole left by the mold as above and fill the mold with warm wax. Cool the candle completely, then unmold it as above.

Candles can be wrapped in cellophane or brown paper. Or package them in a small basket or box lined with excelsior.

Years ago Dad would cut short hunks of log as a base for pillar candles, then decorate them with sprigs of evergreen.

I like using unusual objects as candleholders. These red votive candles look terrific in an antique muffin tin.

49

The Holiday Punch Bowl

Mulled Cider-Brandy Wassail Bowl

Teetotalers' Tea Punch

Victorian Rum Punch

Syllabub

Gingered Red Wine Wassail Bowl

Big Batch Bloody Marys

Sherried Eggnog

Somehow, in a world where even one punch bowl may be more than anyone really *needs,* I've managed to acquire a few. When I go to tag sales or flea markets, I always get ribbed about needing just one more (I haven't taken an accurate inventory lately, but I believe I really only have five or six).

But sometimes I see one I can't resist, like the bowl pictured opposite. Six or seven years ago, at a tag sale in Connecticut, I stumbled onto this set, still in its original box with the platter and all the cups intact, which had been a wedding gift half a century earlier—for twenty dollars, who could pass it up? A few months later I saw an identical bowl in a rather fancy antiques shop in New York's Hudson Valley. The tag declared that this very bowl had once belonged to Eleanor Roosevelt and it declared a nice steep price as well. Since then my tag sale bowl has been referred to as the Eleanor Roosevelt Punch Bowl.

As I said earlier, you don't *need* a punch bowl—any large container, from a bread bowl to a big glass or stoneware crock, can be brought into service. But a real punch bowl, even if it was never owned by a First Lady, will do nicely, too.

Mulled Cider-Brandy Wassail Bowl

* * *

MAKES 40 TO 50 SERVINGS

I've been serving this warming brew every year at my holiday open house, ladled right from a big kettle on the stove. It's easy to make and, even more important, easy to replenish. For a lighter drink, omit the brandy.

1 gallon freshly pressed apple cider
8 cinnamon sticks
1 tablespoon whole allspice
1 tablespoon whole cloves
1 orange, sliced horizontally
1 lemon, sliced horizontally
1 gallon good-quality dry white jug wine
2 cups brandy

1. Combine the cider, spices, and fruit in a stockpot large enough to hold all the ingredients. Place the pot over medium heat and bring to a simmer. Turn the heat down as low as possible and allow the mixture to mull for about an hour.

2. About 10 minutes before serving, pour the wine and brandy into the pot and stir well. Allow the mixture to warm through before serving.

Teetotalers' Tea Punch

* * *

MAKES ABOUT 16 SERVINGS

4 tablespoons light brown sugar
2 cinnamon sticks, broken in half
2 quarts (8 cups) boiling water
4 orange pekoe tea bags
2 cups each pineapple juice, white grape
   juice, and strained orange juice,
   heated to simmering

Combine the brown sugar and cinnamon in a large teapot or other heatproof, nonmetallic vessel. Pour the boiling water over all and stir to dissolve the sugar. Add the tea bags, cover, and steep 5 minutes. Pour the mixture into a punch bowl, remove the tea bags, and stir in the juices.

Served in the famous "Eleanor Roosevelt" punch bowl, Teetotalers' Tea Punch is garnished with slices of star fruit.

Rum punch is served from a hand-stenciled crock I bought at a craft fair. The Santa mugs are from the fifties.

Victorian Rum Punch

✳ ✳ ✳

MAKES ABOUT 24 SERVINGS

1 teaspoon whole allspice
2 small cinnamon sticks, broken in half
2 quarts fresh apple cider
2 quarts white grape juice
1 teaspoon Angostura bitters
½ cup sugar
1½ cups dark rum

Garnish

Whole cloves
4 clementines or 3 tangerines

1. Make a spice bag by tying up the allspice and cinnamon in a double layer of cheesecloth. Place the spice bag in a large kettle and add the cider, grape juice, bitters, and sugar. Place the pan over medium-low heat and stir until the sugar is dissolved. Bring to a simmer, reduce the heat to low, and simmer for 1 hour.

2. Remove the pan from the heat and discard the spice bag. Carefully pour the punch into a punch bowl and stir in the rum.

3. To garnish the punch, press whole cloves into clementines and float the fruit in the punch. Serve the punch warm.

Syllabub

✳ ✳ ✳

MAKES ABOUT 20 SERVINGS

Years ago, milk punches were extremely popular in England and America, especially at holiday time. Syllabub, a medieval English punch made with cider and spices, is an eggless but just as festive alternative to eggnog Stir an ounce of rum or Madeira into each serving if you'd like.

1½ cups milk
1½ cups sugar
2 quarts freshly pressed apple cider
2 teaspoons vanilla extract
¼ teaspoon salt
2 pints heavy cream
Nutmeg, for garnish

1. In a large mixing bowl, combine all the ingredients except the cream and nutmeg and whisk until the sugar is dissolved. In a separate chilled bowl, whip the cream until stiff. (*The punch can be prepared several hours in advance up to this point. Refrigerate the cider mixture and the whipped cream separately.*)

2. Just before serving, combine the cider mixture and the whipped cream in a punch bowl and whisk just until smooth. Garnish with a generous grating of nutmeg.

Gingered Red Wine Wassail Bowl

❋ ❋ ❋

M A K E S   A B O U T   2 0   S E R V I N G S

4 cups cranberry juice cocktail
4 cups pineapple juice
1 1-inch knob fresh gingerroot
1 teaspoon whole allspice
2 cinnamon sticks, broken in half
2 750-milliliter bottles dry red wine
1 orange, sliced horizontally
1 apple, thinly sliced

1. Combine the juices, ginger, allspice, and cinnamon in a stockpot large enough to hold all the ingredients. Place the pot over medium heat and bring to a simmer. Turn the heat down as low as possible and allow the mixture to mull for about an hour.

2. About 10 minutes before serving, pour the wine into the pot, stir well, and add the orange and apple slices. Allow the mixture to warm through before serving.

A red wine wassail looks great in this big spongeware bowl (top). Syllabub is ladled from a big old yellow-ware bread bowl into ribbon-tied mugs (above).

When I'm having a crowd, I let guests serve themselves by ladling Bloody Marys from a big 2-gallon glass crock.

Big Batch Bloody Marys

* * *

MAKES ABOUT 30 SERVINGS

At my holiday open house I always offer Bloody Marys, and it's a lot easier to have a big batch already mixed up rather than making one drink at a time. The vodka is added to each individual serving (or not at all) to suit each guest's taste.

2 46-ounce cans tomato juice
1 46-ounce can vegetable juice (such as V-8)
Juice of 1 lemon
Juice of 1 orange
¼ cup prepared horseradish

½ cup Worcestershire sauce
2 teaspoons freshly ground black pepper
1 tablespoon hot pepper sauce
Vodka (optional)
Lime wedges and whole scallions, for garnish

In a large pot or crock, combine the juices, horseradish, Worcestershire, pepper, and hot pepper sauce and mix well. Ladle the mixture into glasses over ice, with or without an ounce of vodka per serving. Garnish each drink with a lime wedge or a scallion.

Sherried Eggnog

* * *

MAKES 12 SERVINGS

This eggnog has no raw yolks, but is rather a thin cooked custard, flavored with vanilla, sherry, and a dash of freshly grated nutmeg.

2½ pints heavy cream
½ pint half-and-half
12 large eggs, separated
1¼ cups sugar
¾ cup dry sherry
1 teaspoon vanilla extract
Pinch of salt
Nutmeg, for garnish

1. In a large, heavy saucepan, combine 2 pints of the heavy cream and the half-and-half. Place the pan over low heat and heat until just below the simmering point.

2. In a mixing bowl, whisk the egg yolks and 1 cup sugar and beat until blended. Gradually whisk the hot cream mixture into the egg mixture. Pour the mixture back into the saucepan and place over low heat. Cook, stirring constantly, until the mixture thickens and coats the back of a spoon, about 10 minutes. Remove from the heat, allow to cool, and stir in the sherry and vanilla. (*Can be made a day in advance up to this point, cooled, then refrigerated, tightly covered with plastic wrap.*)

3. In a clean bowl, beat the egg whites until soft peaks form. In a separate bowl, beat the remain-

ing ½ pint cream until soft peaks form, then beat in the salt and the remaining ¼ cup sugar. Fold the egg white mixture into the cream mixture.

4. To serve, pour the chilled eggnog mixture into a punch bowl, then mound the egg white-cream mixture on top. Garnish with a generous grating of nutmeg.

Irish Eggnog My friends Jonni and Joe Ryder put an unusual twist on eggnog—they make it with Irish whiskey rather than sherry.

Eggnog, served from a Chinese bowl into flea market coffee cups, really needs to be "drunk" with a spoon.
My artist friend Lisa Begin painted the mats and framed the antique Christmas postcards in the background.

A Christmas Week Open House

MENU FOR 30

Mulled Cider-Brandy Wassail Bowl
(page 50)

Teetotalers' Tea Punch (page 51)

*

Currant-Glazed Country Ham

Cherry Ketchup (page 10)

Bourbon Jelly (page 9)

Pecan-Herb Biscuits

Scallion Corn Muffins

Eggplant Caviar Provençale

Chicken Liver Pâté with Calvados
and Hazelnuts

Mediterranean White Bean Spread
with Rosemary

Assorted Toasts

Shrimp and Lobster Mousse
with Cucumbers and Sugar Snap Peas

Cheddar and Chutney Tarts

*

German Chocolate Brownies

Little Banana Pies
in Almond Crusts

Christmas Cookies

A Bowl of Winter Fruit

The Christmas season is the appropriate time of the year to get together with budding new friends and to once again gather my oldest friends together. One of my annual traditions is to host a late-afternoon open house on New Year's Day; when I'm out on tour with a new book or lecturing, I meet many new friends and when I'm having a nice conversation with someone, I often impulsively invite them to "stop by on New Year's Day." Sometime between Christmas and New Year's I panic—what possessed me to invite so many people? And what would happen if everyone I invited actually *showed up?* Of course, this never happens, but some of these

Little votive candles and silver ribbons strung among the baskets, bowls, and platters add sparkle to the buffet table.

new friends *have* shown up and have now become old friends.

Just as with my guest list, there are always a few changes to the menu, and the menu here is the most recent one. In order to be a guest at one's own party, it's best to have some help, and this year I hired a young student couple to help make drinks, wash glasses, serve, and keep the buffet table replenished and tidy. I established

another custom this year—as everyone came inside each guest was given a name tag, and before the day was over new friends had made friends with the old ones. It was a good party and, of course, I now have a whole year to meet more new friends and add to my guest list.

GETTING READY There's a lot to do here, but nothing's difficult. Dividing the work over a few days makes it all a little bit easier.

The condiments for the ham (Cherry Ketchup and Bourbon Jelly) can be made well in advance. The Cheddar and Chutney Tarts can also be made well ahead and frozen, tightly wrapped; thaw them before baking. The biscuits and muffins can also be made well in advance and frozen (otherwise, they're best made no sooner than the day before they are to be served).

Two or three days before the party, make the eggplant caviar and the white bean spread, cover them tightly, and store in the refrigerator. For serving with the spreads, toast thin slices of assorted breads in a low oven; pack them in tightly covered containers. Up to two days in advance, make the banana pies and store them in tins in a cool place.

The day before the party, precook the ham and make the Shrimp and Lobster Mousse and the brownies. The chicken liver pâté can be made a day before the party, but no sooner.

Early on the day of the party, prepare the cucumbers and sugar snap peas for the mousse and the endive leaves for the eggplant caviar. Mull the cider and mix the punches. About a half hour before the party, start setting up the table.

Currant-Glazed Country Ham

✳ ✳ ✳

SERVES A CROWD AS AN HORS D'OEUVRE

I do a ham of one kind or another every year for my open house. Last year, my friend Emyl Jenkins, author of *Southern Christmas,* sent me a country ham from her home state of Virginia, and I got all the raves. This year, another friend, Sharron Barker, who teaches cooking down Louisville way, insisted I try one of the justly famous hams of Kentucky. I'm not going to get involved in any competition here—you decide where your ham is going to come from.

The ham takes a little time to prepare (start at least a day in advance, following the instructions on the ham's cloth sack), but not a lot of work, and believe me, it's worth it.

For a party, I serve the richly flavored ham carved into little slivers with little biscuits and muffins and several condiments alongside.

1 country ham (about 12 pounds), cooked
Whole cloves
¾ cup currant jelly, melted, approximately

1. To bake and glaze the ham, preheat the oven to 300°F. Remove the ham from the refrigerator, unwrap it, and place it on a rack in a shallow roasting pan, flatter side down. Diagonally score the layer of fat, being careful not to cut into the meat itself. Stud the ham with cloves, then brush a thin layer of the melted jelly over the surface.

2. Bake the ham, brushing with more jelly as necessary, until heated through and well glazed, about an hour. Serve the ham warm or at room temperature, carved into small slivers.

Pecan-Herb Biscuits

* * *

MAKES 2 TO 3 DOZEN,
DEPENDING ON THE SIZE
OF THE CUTTERS

1¾ *cups unbleached all-purpose flour*
½ *teaspoon salt*
1 *tablespoon baking powder*
⅓ *cup chilled vegetable shortening*
¾ *cup milk*
2 *tablespoons chopped parsley*
2 *tablespoons snipped chives*
½ *teaspoon dried thyme*
½ *teaspoon dried sage*
¼ *cup finely chopped pecans*

1. Preheat the oven to 400°F.

2. In a mixing bowl, sift together the flour, salt, and baking powder. Using a pastry blender or 2 knives, cut in the shortening until the mixture resembles coarse meal.

3. Add the milk and mix with a fork until just blended. Add the parsley, chives, thyme, sage, and pecans and mix well.

4. On a lightly floured surface, pat the dough out to a thickness of about ½ inch. Using a lightly floured small biscuit cutter, cut out the biscuits (or cut the dough into 1½-inch squares).

5. Place the biscuits about an inch apart on an ungreased baking sheet. Bake until the biscuits are golden brown, about 12 minutes. Serve hot, or remove to wire racks to cool and serve at room temperature. (*The biscuits can be made a day in advance, slightly underbaked, and stored in a tightly covered container, or made up to 2 weeks in advance and frozen, tightly wrapped; in either case, refresh them by placing in a moderate oven for a few minutes.*)

Scallion Corn Muffins

* * *

MAKES 3 DOZEN
MINIATURE MUFFINS

¾ *cup unbleached all-purpose flour*
1¼ *cups stone-ground yellow cornmeal*
2½ *teaspoons baking powder*
½ *teaspoon salt*
2 *tablespoons firmly packed light brown sugar*
3 *scallions, white and green parts, finely chopped*
1 *large egg, lightly beaten*
2 *tablespoons unsalted butter, melted*
1 *cup lowfat milk*

1. Preheat the oven to 400°F. Lightly grease 3 miniature muffin tins (or use nonstick tins).

2. In a mixing bowl, sift together the flour, cornmeal, baking powder, salt, and brown sugar. Add the remaining ingredients all at once and mix with a fork until the dry ingredients are just moistened, making a somewhat lumpy batter.

3. Spoon the batter into the prepared muffin tins, filling the cups about ⅔ full. Place the pans in the oven and bake until the muffins are risen and lightly browned at the edges, about 15 to 20 minutes. (*The muffins can be made up to a day in advance and stored in a tightly covered container, or made up to 2 weeks in advance and frozen.*)

Spreads seem more "fancy" served in old footed compotes.

Eggplant Caviar Provençale

✳ ✳ ✳

MAKES ABOUT 4 CUPS

This simple version of eggplant caviar from Southern France is less well known than its Southern Italian cousin, but its simplicity lets the smoky flavor of eggplant really shine. Make it a day in advance to allow the flavors to blend and mellow. Garnish the caviar with chopped parsley and lemon slices and serve it with endive leaves.

> *2 medium eggplants (about 2 pounds)*
> *1 small onion, finely chopped*
> *6 large garlic cloves, finely chopped*
> *3 tablespoons capers, chopped*
> *6 anchovy fillets, drained, rinsed well, and*
> *   mashed*
> *2 tablespoons extra virgin olive oil*

> *¼ cup lemon juice*
> *¼ cup chopped parsley*
> *Salt and freshly ground black pepper*
> *2 endives, washed and separated into*
> *   leaves, for serving*

1. Preheat the broiler. Cut the eggplants in half lengthwise, then puncture the skin all over with a sharp fork. Place the eggplant, cut-side down, on a lightly oiled baking sheet and broil until the skin is charred and the eggplant has begun to collapse, about 10 minutes. Remove the eggplant from the heat and allow it to become cool enough to handle.

2. Using a large spoon, scoop the eggplant pulp into a mixing bowl and discard the skin. Add the onion, garlic, capers, anchovies, oil, lemon juice, and parsley to the bowl and mash with a fork until the mixture is fairly smooth. Season with salt and plenty of pepper. Cover and refrigerate overnight to allow the flavors to mellow. (*The caviar can be made up to 2 days in advance.*)

3. Serve the caviar in a bowl, garnished with additional chopped parsley and lemon wedges. Poke the endive leaves, stem-side down, around the edges of the caviar.

Chicken Liver Pâté with Calvados and Hazelnuts

✳ ✳ ✳

MAKES ABOUT 4 CUPS

Even though this wonderfully flavored pâté is *very* rich it seems to disappear quickly, so I always make a big batch. I serve this with toasted thin slices of pumpernickel or apple slices

that have been rubbed with a cut lemon to prevent browning.

¼ pound bacon, finely chopped
½ cup (1 stick) unsalted butter, softened
3 large garlic cloves, chopped
1 medium onion, coarsely chopped
1 baking apple, pared and coarsely
*   chopped*
2 pounds chicken livers
¼ teaspoon salt
⅛ teaspoon cayenne pepper
⅛ teaspoon freshly ground black pepper
¼ teaspoon grated nutmeg
¼ teaspoon ground allspice
⅓ cup Calvados or applejack
½ cup finely chopped hazelnuts, lightly
*   toasted*

1. Put the bacon in a large, heavy skillet and
place over medium heat. When the bacon begins
to render its fat, add 2 tablespoons of the butter,
the garlic, onion, and apple and sauté until
the onion is nicely browned, about 15 minutes.
Add the livers and sauté until brown on the
outside but still slightly pink on the inside, 5
to 7 minutes.

2. Transfer the mixture to the bowl of a food
processor fitted with the steel chopping blade.
Add the salt, spices, and the remaining butter and
process until the mixture is smooth. Stir in the
Calvados and hazelnuts. Transfer the mixture to
a bowl and cover with plastic wrap, pressing the
wrap directly onto the surface of the pâté.

3. Refrigerate 6 hours or overnight to allow the
flavors to blend. (*The pâté can be made a day in
advance, but no sooner.*)

Mediterranean White Bean Spread with Rosemary

* * *

MAKES 3½ CUPS

*T*his may be one of the shortest and
quickest recipes you'll ever find anywhere.
Serve the spread with little hunks of sourdough
bread or strips of toasted pita.

2 16-ounce cans cannellini (white kidney
*   beans, see Note), drained and rinsed*
1 garlic clove, chopped
¼ cup extra virgin olive oil
1 tablespoon lemon juice
1½ teaspoons dried or 2 tablespoons fresh
*   rosemary leaves*
¼ cup flat-leaf parsley leaves
1 teaspoon mild paprika
Salt and hot pepper sauce
Lemon wedges, for garnish

Combine all the ingredients except the salt
and pepper sauce in the bowl of a food processor
fitted with the steel chopping blade and process
until smooth. Season to taste with salt and plenty
of hot pepper sauce. Transfer to a bowl or jar,
cover tightly, and refrigerate up to 4 days.
Garnish with lemon wedges before serving.

NOTE Cannellini seems to be one product that is
not canned in consistent sizes. Depending on the
maker, cans that are 15, 16, and even 19 ounces
can be found in the market. This is not a scientif-
ically exact recipe anyway, so use whatever size
cans you find and adjust the amount of oil and
seasonings if necessary.

Shrimp and Lobster Mousse

✳ ✳ ✳

SERVES 20 AS AN
HORS D'OEUVRE

A few steps (and a few dirtied bowls) are involved here, but the end result is worth it. Serve the mousse with steamed and chilled sugar snap peas, slices of cucumber, or small thin slices of black bread.

1½ tablespoons unsalted butter
1½ tablespoons unbleached all-purpose flour

I make a seafood mousse of one kind or another every year, and I always serve it on a big silverplate platter.

1 cup milk
2 tablespoons (2 envelopes) unflavored gelatin
⅓ cup cold water
⅓ cup boiling water
1 cup mayonnaise
¼ cup tomato paste
2 tablespoons lemon juice
1 tablespoon prepared horseradish
½ teaspoon salt
½ teaspoon red pepper sauce (Tabasco), or more to taste
1 celery stalk, coarsely chopped
1 small onion, coarsely chopped
½ pound cooked shrimp, peeled and deveined
1 pound cooked lobster meat, flaked
1 cup (½ pint) heavy cream

1. In a small, heavy saucepan, melt the butter over low heat. Whisk in the flour until well blended, then slowly whisk in the milk. Continue cooking, whisking constantly, until the sauce thickens, 3 to 5 minutes. Remove from the heat and cool.

2. In a large mixing bowl, whisk together the gelatin and cold water to soften the gelatin, then whisk in the boiling water to dissolve it.

3. In the bowl of a food processor fitted with the steel chopping blade (or in a blender), combine the mayonnaise, tomato paste, lemon juice, horseradish, salt, Tabasco, celery, onion, and shrimp and process until smooth. Stir this mixture into the gelatin mixture, then stir in the cooled sauce from step 1. Stir in the lobster.

4. In another clean bowl (sorry!), whip the

heavy cream until soft peaks form, then fold the whipped cream into the lobster mixture.

5. Lightly oil two 3½- to 4-cup molds and spoon the mousse mixture into them. Chill until firm, then cover each of the molds with plastic wrap until serving.

6. To serve, dip a mold into a basin of warm water just long enough to loosen the mousse. Invert the mousse onto a serving platter and surround it with the vegetables or bread.

Cheddar and Chutney Tarts

* * *

MAKES ABOUT 4 DOZEN

I always like to have one or two hot hors d'oeuvres that are passed, since it's a nice surprise when a trayful of some little morsel appears before the guests. These are especially easy since they're made in advance and all that needs to be done just before serving time is the baking.

½ cup (¼ pound) finely grated sharp Cheddar cheese
2 3-ounce packages cream cheese, softened
1 teaspoon curry powder
⅓ cup finely chopped Major Grey's chutney
4 scallions, white and green parts, finely chopped
2 sheets (1 17½-ounce package) frozen puff pastry, thawed in the refrigerator

1. In a small bowl, combine the cheeses

These little tartlets offer an interesting flavor combination.

and curry powder and mix well. Stir in the chutney and scallions. Set aside. (*The filling can be made several days in advance and stored in the refrigerator.*)

2. One sheet at a time, unfold the pastry onto a lightly floured work surface. Cut the pastry into 2-inch squares and press the squares into the cups of miniature muffin pans, then prick the dough with a fork. Place a scant teaspoonful of the cheese mixture in each square. (*The tarts can be made a day in advance up to this point, wrapped well, and refrigerated, or made well in advance and frozen.*)

3. Preheat the oven to 400°F. Bake until the pastry is golden brown, about 15 minutes. Serve warm.

German Chocolate Brownies

* * *

MAKES ABOUT 42.

Brownies are either soft and fudgy or firmer and more cakelike. For a plain brownie I usually prefer the former, but here the more cakelike version is the perfect foil for the crunchy and gooey frosting. It's okay to substitute vegetable shortening for the butter in the batter, but for the best flavor, do use butter in the frosting.

½ cup (1 stick) unsalted butter
4 ounces (4 squares) semisweet chocolate
1 cup granulated sugar
2 large eggs
1 teaspoon vanilla extract
1½ cups unbleached all-purpose flour
¼ teaspoon salt

Frosting

½ cup firmly packed dark brown sugar
¼ cup (½ stick) unsalted butter
½ cup evaporated milk
2 large egg yolks
½ teaspoon vanilla extract
⅔ cup chopped pecans, lightly toasted
1 cup shredded coconut

1. Preheat the oven to 350°F. Lightly grease a 9 x 13-inch cake pan.

2. In a heavy, medium saucepan, melt the butter over low heat. Add the chocolate and stir occasionally until it is melted. Remove the pan from the heat and stir in the sugar. Using a large spoon, beat in the eggs until well blended, then beat in the vanilla. Stir in the flour and salt.

3. Transfer the batter to the prepared pan and bake until the edges start to come away from the pan and a cake tester or wooden skewer inserted in the center comes out clean, about 25 minutes. Transfer the pan to a wire rack and cool in the pan.

4. To make the frosting, combine the sugar, butter, evaporated milk, and egg yolks in a small, heavy saucepan and place over low heat. Cook, stirring frequently, until the mixture is thickened, 10 to 12 minutes. Remove from the heat, beat in the vanilla, and continue beating until the mixture is a soft, spreadable consistency. Stir in the pecans and coconut.

5. Spread the frosting evenly over the cooled cake and allow it to become cool and firm. Cut the cake into 1½-inch squares. (*The brownies can be made up to 2 days in advance and packed in tightly covered containers with wax paper between the layers. Store in a cool place.*)

Little Banana Pies in Almond Crusts

* * *

MAKES ABOUT 3 DOZEN TARTLETS

The smooth filling in these little tarts contrasts quite nicely with the crunch of the crust. For the best banana flavor be sure to have very, *very* ripe bananas.

Crust

1 cup (2 sticks) unsalted butter, softened
3 cups unbleached all-purpose flour
¼ teaspoon salt

⅓ cup granulated sugar
½ teaspoon vanilla extract
½ teaspoon almond extract
¾ cup finely chopped almonds

Filling

2 large eggs
1 cup firmly packed light brown sugar
½ teaspoon vanilla extract
1 tablespoon unbleached all-purpose flour
¼ teaspoon salt
1 teaspoon ground cinnamon
Grated rind of 1 small orange
3 very ripe bananas, peeled and mashed
½ cup sliced almonds, approximately
Confectioners' sugar, for garnish

1. To make the crust, combine the butter, flour, salt, granulated sugar, and extracts in a large mixing bowl and knead until evenly blended, then knead in the chopped almonds. Press walnut-sized pieces of dough into 2-inch miniature muffin cups, lining the bottoms and sides. Set aside.

2. Preheat the oven to 350°F.

3. To make the filling, combine the eggs and brown sugar in a mixing bowl and beat until smooth. Beat in all the remaining ingredients except the sliced almonds. Spoon the filling into the crust-lined muffin cups and sprinkle a few almond slices onto each tartlet.

4. Bake until the filling is set and browned at the edges, 25 to 30 minutes. Remove the pans to wire racks and allow the tarts to cool before removing them from the pans. Store the tarts in tightly covered containers up to 2 days in a cool place. Dust with confectioners' sugar before serving.

THE BUFFET TABLE

❋

A little advance preparation makes the last-minute preparations before the party relatively painless. I always set out my serving dishes the night before, a sort of "dress rehearsal," giving me plenty of time to change my mind and rearrange things if I want to. Then a slip of paper goes into each platter, bowl, or basket with the name of the food to be served from them.

I like to garnish everything simply but lavishly, using curly lettuces, radicchio, lemon leaves (available from the florist), and herbs, so when I make my shopping list, I include those as well. When garnishing, it's best to keep the decorative elements toward the outer edges of the food so everything stays neater.

For buffets I like sweets that are no more than a mouthful.

A Carolers' Supper

MENU FOR 8

Christmas Eve Seafood Soup

Sourdough Toasts

∗

Apple and Apricot Brown Betty

Wonderful Christmas Eve traditions abound in small towns all over the country. In nearby Basking Ridge here in New Jersey, the townspeople hold an annual carol sing alongside the big Christmas tree in the historic town square, a tradition that began over seventy years ago. At around seven in the evening, the crowd begins to arrive on foot, wearing their holiday finery (Santa

hats and faux antlers are very much evident), and a very convincing Santa wanders through the crowd handing out candy canes. At seven-thirty, the caroling begins. From the front steps of the Greek Revival Presbyterian church, a brass choir made up of local citizens accompanies the crowd, and at the end, to the final strains of "Hark, the Herald Angels Sing," the ancient church bells peal. Talk about Christmas spirit!

Larry Terricone lives just down the hill from the town square, and after the spirit-lifting carol sing a group of us strolled happily back to his cozy c.1830 clapboard house, Grey Cottage, to share this warming supper.

GETTING READY If the soup is made up to a day in advance, there's virtually no last-minute preparation involved here, except for warming it up. Up to a few days in advance, brush thin slices of sourdough baguette lightly with olive oil and toast them in a slow oven; store in tightly covered containers. The dessert is best made no sooner than early on the day it is to be served.

Henrietta, Diane O'Connor's stuffed giraffe (left), does some appropriate Christmas Eve reading.

Even a simple meal like this one becomes special when the table is set with care. Here, a bowl of antique velvet fruit serves as the centerpiece. The room is decorated to the nines, with greenery and little angels hanging from the chandelier.

The simple seafood soup (left) is served with lightly toasted slices of sourdough baguette and garnished with sprigs of parsley.

Christmas Eve Seafood Soup

* * *

SERVES 6 TO 8

*I*f fish on Christmas Eve is a tradition in your family but time is at a premium, this creamy soup that combines shrimp, halibut, and scallops is the answer.

4 tablespoons (½ stick) unsalted butter
1 medium onion, chopped
1 celery stalk, with leaves, finely chopped
2 garlic cloves, chopped
3 cups well-seasoned fish stock (see Note)
1 cup dry white wine
2 tablespoons brandy (optional)
2 bay leaves
½ teaspoon dried thyme
1 pound medium shrimp, peeled and
*   deveined*
1 pound halibut or other firm, white fish,
*   cut into chunks*
1 pound bay scallops
2 tablespoons unbleached all-purpose flour
2 cups milk
2 tablespoons chopped parsley
Parsley sprigs, for garnish

1. Melt the butter in a Dutch oven or heavy soup kettle. Add the onion, celery, and garlic and sauté over medium-low heat until golden, 7 to 10 minutes.

2. Add the stock, wine, brandy, bay leaves, and thyme and simmer 20 minutes. Stir in the shrimp, halibut, and scallops and simmer just until the fish is opaque, about 5 minutes longer.

3. Spoon about ½ cup of the broth into a small bowl and whisk in the flour. Stir this mixture into the kettle, bring the soup to a simmer, and cook until the broth thickens, about 5 minutes. Stir in the milk and parsley and heat to just below the simmering point. (*The soup can be made up to a day in advance and refrigerated.*) Serve hot, garnished with parsley sprigs, with toasted slices of sourdough bread alongside.

NOTE Two cups (two 8-ounce bottles) clam juice and 1 cup water can be substituted for the stock.

Apple and Apricot Brown Betty

* * *

SERVES 6

1 cup dried apricot halves
1½ cups coarse, soft fresh bread crumbs
½ cup (1 stick) unsalted butter, melted
1 cup sugar
⅛ teaspoon salt
½ teaspoon ground cinnamon
½ teaspoon ground ginger
¼ teaspoon grated nutmeg
½ teaspoon grated lemon rind
4 large baking apples, such as Granny
*   Smith or yellow Delicious, peeled,*
*   quartered, and cored*
1 pint vanilla ice cream, slightly softened

1. In a small saucepan, combine the apricot halves with water to barely cover, then place over medium heat. Bring to a boil, reduce the heat to low, and simmer 5 minutes. Remove from the heat and allow to cool.

Even a humble dessert like this brown betty is festive when served in goblets set onto beautiful little plates.

2. Preheat the oven to 350°F. Lightly grease a shallow 2-quart baking pan.

3. In a mixing bowl, combine the bread crumbs and butter and toss well. In a separate small bowl, combine the sugar, salt, spices, and lemon rind. Add the bread crumbs and butter and toss well. Spread half the crumb mixture evenly over the bottom of the pan.

4. Arrange the apple quarters in an even layer over the crumbs in the pan, then, using a slotted spoon, spoon the apricots over the apples. Spread the remaining crumb mixture over the fruit and drizzle any remaining apricot liquid over the crumbs.

5. Cover the baking dish with aluminum foil and bake until the apples are barely tender, about 30 minutes. Remove the cover, raise the heat, and bake until the crumbs are nicely browned, about 12 minutes longer.

6. Spoon the warm betty (if made in advance, rewarm for 15 minutes in a low oven) into individual serving dishes and top each serving with a big dab of softened vanilla ice cream.

REINDEER CHOW
*

Everyone remembers to put out a plate of cookies for Santa on Christmas Eve, but we tend to forget about his reindeer, without whom he'd still be stuck up at the North Pole. The Girl Scouts of Fair Haven, New Jersey, haven't forgotten Santa's friends and they've established a wonderful custom. Small brown paper bags filled with a handful of hay are distributed throughout the community. Each bag is tied up with a card that's inscribed with this poem:

It's Christmas in Fair Haven and Santa is here.
To remind us to leave treats for his favorite reindeer.
Cookies and milk are great for Saint Nick
And "chow" for the reindeer will just do the trick.
Just sprinkle some chow on your lawn before bed
And soon Santa will come with reindeer and sled.

(Here in Chatham, there's only one little problem with setting out chow for Santa's reindeer. Our own local deer will have the chow all polished off long before Donder, Blitzen, and Rudolph ever have a chance!)

A Simple but Hearty Supper

Broccoli and Red Pepper Salad with Lemon-Balsamic Vinaigrette

Fettuccine with Walnut Cream Sauce

*

Pears Poached in Port and Cointreau with Ginger Pound Cake

Preparing something good to eat on Christmas Eve should be as painless as possible, and this menu was devised with just that in mind. Everyone loves pasta and this unusual sauce is easy to fix. (If there are picky kids in the group, make a little extra pasta and serve it with a plain tomato sauce or a little butter and grated cheese.) And even a simple meal such as this one can be served in an elegant way.

GETTING READY The pound cake can be made a few weeks in advance and frozen, or bake it up to a day in advance. The pears can be made a day, or two, in advance and refrigerated.

Make the salad the evening before or early on Christmas Eve day. The sauce for the pasta can be made early in the day and refrigerated; bring to room temperature before mixing with the hot pasta.

Broccoli and Red Pepper Salad with Lemon-Balsamic Vinaigrette

* * *

SERVES 6 TO 8

Lemon-Balsamic Vinaigrette
½ cup extra virgin olive oil
2 tablespoons balsamic vinegar
Juice of 1 lemon
1 garlic clove, crushed
Salt and freshly ground black pepper
*   to taste*

2 large bunches broccoli, cut into 3-inch
*   spears (reserve stalk ends for soup or*
*   another use)*
4 roasted red peppers, cut into strips

1. Combine the dressing ingredients in a jar, shake well, cover, and refrigerate for 2 or 3 hours.

2. Place the broccoli in a vegetable steamer over simmering water, cover, and steam until the broccoli is crisp-tender and bright green. When done, rinse briefly under cold water to stop cooking.

3. Place the warm broccoli and the pepper strips in a serving bowl. Remove the garlic from the dressing and pour the dressing over the vegetables. Toss the salad and refrigerate up to 24 hours. Remove from the refrigerator about an hour before serving and serve at room temperature.

The table is set with old damask linens, cobalt glass dishes, and an assortment of stemware, with Toothpick Trees (page 38) and a few silvery balls as a centerpiece. At right, the simple but colorful main course.

Fettuccine with Walnut Cream Sauce

* * *

SERVES 6 TO 8

1¼ cups walnut pieces
3 tablespoons pignoli (pine nuts)
1½ pounds dried fettuccine or tagliatelle
1 cup frozen green peas, thawed (optional)
2 large garlic cloves
½ cup parsley leaves
2 tablespoons fine, dry bread crumbs
1 cup milk or light cream
2 tablespoons olive oil
2 tablespoons unsalted butter, softened
½ cup grated Romano or Parmesan
    cheese, plus more for passing at the
    table
Parsley sprigs, for garnish

1. Preheat the oven to 300°F. Spread the walnuts and pignoli in an even layer on a baking sheet. Bake until the nuts are lightly toasted, 7 to 10 minutes. Remove from the oven and cool.

2. Meanwhile, place a large kettle of salted water over high heat and bring to a boil. Add the pasta, reduce the heat to medium, and cook until the pasta is al dente. In a separate small pan, cook the peas if using in salted water to cover until crisp-tender.

3. In the bowl of a food processor fitted with the steel chopping blade, combine all but ¼ cup of the nut mixture with the garlic, parsley, bread crumbs, milk, oil, butter, and cheese. Process the mixture until the nuts are very finely chopped.

4. Drain the cooked pasta, return it to the pot, and add the sauce and the peas. Toss the pasta to coat it evenly with the sauce and transfer to individual serving dishes immediately.

5. Sprinkle each serving with grated cheese, then garnish each serving with some of the reserved nuts, a sprig of parsley, and a grinding of pepper. Pass more grated cheese at the table.

Pears Poached in Port and Cointreau

* * *

SERVES 8

3 cups ruby port
½ cup Cointreau liqueur
2 cups sugar
2 tablespoons chopped gingerroot
2 4-inch cinnamon sticks, broken in half
1 teaspoon whole cloves
8 firm ripe pears, peeled but with stems
    left on
1 teaspoon vanilla extract
Mint sprigs, for garnish

1. In a large saucepan with a lid, combine the port, Cointreau, sugar, ginger, cinnamon sticks, and cloves. Place over medium-high heat and bring to a boil, stirring until the sugar is dissolved. Reduce the heat to low and simmer for 10 minutes. Remove from the heat.

2. As each pear is peeled, use tongs to drop it into the syrup. When all the pears are in the pan, return it to the heat and bring the syrup to a simmer again. Cover the pan loosely and simmer until the pears are tender but not mushy, about 20 minutes.

3. Using the tongs or a slotted spoon, remove the pears from the hot syrup and place them upright in a shallow 2-quart baking dish.

4. Simmer the syrup until it is reduced by half, 15 to 20 minutes, then stir in the vanilla. Pour the syrup through a sieve over the pears and allow to cool. Cover the dish tightly with plastic wrap and chill 4 hours or overnight.

5. Serve the pears in footed glasses with a little syrup spooned over them. Garnish each with a sprig of mint and serve a slice of Ginger Pound Cake alongside.

Ginger Pound Cake

* * *

MAKES TWO 8 1/2 X 4 1/2 - INCH
LOAVES

Two kinds of ginger, ground and preserved, give this simple golden cake its piquancy. I always make two loaves—one for now and one for the freezer. For parties, I cut pound cake in half lengthwise before cutting it into slices.

2 cups (4 sticks) unsalted butter, softened
2 cups sugar
10 large eggs, at room temperature
2 teaspoons vanilla extract
3 1/2 cups unbleached all-purpose flour
1/2 teaspoon baking powder
1/2 teaspoon salt
2 teaspoons ground ginger
1/2 cup finely chopped preserved ginger

1. Preheat the oven to 300°F. Lightly grease two 8 1/2 x 4 1/2-inch loaf pans and dust them lightly with flour.

Pale-colored foods always look wonderful served on jewel-toned dishes like these old cobalt glass plates.

2. In a mixing bowl, cream the butter and sugar together until smooth. Beat in the eggs one at a time, beating well after adding each egg, then beat in the vanilla. In a separate bowl, sift together the flour, baking powder, salt, and ground ginger. A third at a time, beat the dry mixture into the wet mixture, then continue beating at medium speed for 5 minutes.

3. Stir the preserved ginger into the batter, then divide the batter between the 2 prepared pans. Bake until the loaves are nicely browned and a wooden pick or cake tester inserted comes out clean, about 1 hour and 20 to 30 minutes.

4. Transfer the pans to wire racks and cool 10 minutes, then remove the loaves from the pans to cool completely. Wrap the loaves tightly and store in the refrigerator for up to 3 days or in the freezer for up to a month.

Christmas Day Breakfasts

A FEW SUGGESTIONS

Stewed Apricots and Pears

Farmhouse Frittata

Screwdriver Oranges

Carrot and Apple Muffins

Christmastime Marmalade Coffee Cake

Being an old farm boy, mornings are still my favorite time of day. Often on a crisp winter morning, I'll arise with the break of the sun and take my morning coffee with me as I go out onto the back terrace to refill the bird feeders. Then I'll come inside and enjoy my breakfast along with the birds, rabbits, deer, and squirrels.

Christmas Day is the same, except the house is usually full of people. There are a few different suggestions here for serving breakfast on Christmas Day, from something substantial that everyone can sit down to at once to a coffee cake and muffins that are ready whenever the guests arise.

Stewed Apricots and Pears

* * *

SERVES 6

Stewing dried fruits in orange and cranberry juice gives them a little extra flavor as well as a nice tint of color. Serve any leftover stewed fruit over ice cream for an easy dessert.

½ pound dried apricots
½ pound dried pears
1 cup orange juice
1 cup cranberry juice cocktail
1 cup water
1 4-inch cinnamon stick, broken in half
3 or 4 star anise (optional)
½ cup sugar
½ teaspoon vanilla extract

1. In a heavy, medium saucepan, combine the fruit, juices, water, and spices. Place over medium-high heat and bring to a boil. Reduce the heat and simmer until the fruit is tender but not mushy, about 30 minutes.

2. Stir in the sugar and simmer the mixture until it is dissolved, about 5 minutes longer. Remove the pan from the heat and stir in the vanilla. Serve the fruit warm or chilled.

Farmhouse Frittata

* * *

SERVES 6

2 tablespoons unsalted butter
1 tablespoon vegetable oil
4 medium boiling potatoes, quartered and
    sliced
1 small onion, thinly sliced
4 scallions, white and green parts, thinly
    sliced
4 medium button mushrooms, thinly sliced
10 slices Canadian bacon, cut into
    ¼-inch-wide strips
Salt and freshly ground pepper to taste
12 large eggs, lightly beaten
⅓ cup grated Swiss or Parmesan cheese

1. Preheat the oven to 400°F.

2. In a heavy, ovenproof 12-inch skillet, combine the butter and oil and place over medium heat. When the butter is melted, add the potatoes, onion, scallions, mushrooms, and Canadian bacon to the pan and sauté until the onion is golden, about 10 minutes.

3. Remove the skillet from the heat, spread the sautéed vegetables out evenly and season with salt and pepper. Pour the eggs over the vegetables and sprinkle the cheese over all. Place in the preheated oven and bake until the eggs are set and the edges are lightly browned, 25 to 30 minutes.

4. Allow the frittata to cool for 20 minutes or so, then slide the frittata onto a serving dish. Cut into wedges to serve. (*The frittata can be made a day in advance, stored in the refrigerator, and served at room temperature or rewarmed in a low oven.*)

SCREWDRIVER ORANGES

*

This is a simple breakfast idea that's reserved for grown-ups. Allowing 1 orange per person, peel the oranges and slice them horizontally as thin as possible. Place a single layer of slightly overlapping slices in a shallow bowl, sprinkle lightly with confectioners' sugar, and drizzle with vodka and a few drops of Cointreau or Grand Marnier. Repeat twice, then cover tightly and chill a few hours or overnight. Serve cold.

A colorful Farmhouse Frittata, fresh from the oven, can be served directly from the skillet, cut into wedges.

Muffins are great to have on hand to serve any time.

Carrot and Apple Muffins

* * *

MAKES 1 DOZEN

*E*specially moist, these muffins keep well for a few days. Serve them with softened cream cheese and apple butter.

1¼ cups unbleached all-purpose flour
⅔ cup sugar
½ teaspoon salt
1 teaspoon ground cinnamon
1 teaspoon baking soda
1 large egg
½ cup vegetable oil
1 cup shredded carrots
1 yellow Delicious apple, peeled, cored,
    and chopped
Grated rind of 1 lemon
½ cup golden raisins
⅓ cup chopped pecans

1. Preheat the oven to 375°F. Lightly grease a 12-cup muffin pan.

2. In a large mixing bowl, combine the flour, sugar, salt, cinnamon, and baking soda and mix well. Stir in the egg and oil, mixing until the dry ingredients are just moistened, then stir in the carrots, apple, lemon rind, raisins, and pecans.

3. Spoon the batter into the prepared muffin cups. Bake until the muffins are golden brown and a cake tester inserted in one comes out clean, about 30 minutes.

Christmastime Marmalade Coffee Cake

* * *

MAKES ONE 10-INCH
ROUND CAKE

Dough

¼ cup granulated sugar
¼ cup warm tap water
1 envelope active dry yeast
¼ cup (½ stick) unsalted butter
⅔ cup milk
2 large eggs
1 teaspoon vanilla extract
½ teaspoon almond extract
2 to 2½ cups unbleached all-purpose flour

Topping

½ cup unbleached all-purpose flour
⅓ cup firmly packed dark brown sugar
1 teaspoon ground cinnamon
3 tablespoons cold unsalted butter
½ cup sliced almonds

1½ cups Christmastime Marmalade (page 11) or ¾ cup best-quality orange marmalade combined with ¾ cup cranberries

1. In a small bowl, combine 1 tablespoon of the granulated sugar with the warm water, sprinkle the yeast over the mixture, and stir until the yeast is dissolved. Let stand until the mixture becomes frothy, about 10 minutes.

2. Meanwhile, in a small heavy saucepan, combine the butter and milk and place over medium-low heat. Cook, stirring constantly, just until the butter is melted and blended in. Stir in the remaining sugar, then remove from the heat and cool to lukewarm.

3. In a large mixing bowl, combine the yeast mixture, the milk mixture, the eggs, and extracts and beat at low speed until blended. Gradually beat in 2 cups of the flour. Continue beating until the mixture is very smooth, beating in an additional tablespoon of flour at a time to form a soft dough.

4. Cover the bowl with a damp cloth, set it in a warm place, and allow the dough to rise until doubled in bulk, about 1 hour.

5. Meanwhile, prepare the topping. In a small bowl, combine the flour, brown sugar, and cinnamon, then cut in the butter, making coarse crumbs. Stir in the almonds.

6. Preheat the oven to 350°F. Lightly grease a 10-inch tube pan with a removable bottom.

7. Stir the raised dough to deflate it, then spread half of it into the prepared pan. Scatter half the

A colorful cake is a perfect way to start Christmas Day.

marmalade (or marmalade-cranberry mixture) over the dough, then sprinkle half the crumb mixture over the fruit. Repeat with the remaining dough and topping.

8. Bake until the cake is nicely browned and starts to come away from the edge of the pan, 35 to 40 minutes. Place the pan on a wire rack and allow the cake to cool for 15 minutes, then remove the outer ring from the pan. Serve the cake warm or at room temperature. (*The cake can be made well in advance and frozen, tightly wrapped, up to 3 weeks.*)

An Intimate Christmastime Dinner

MENU FOR 6 TO 8

Brussels Sprout and Hazelnut Soup
Parmesan Crackers

*

Roasted Chicken Breasts with Pear,
Scallion, and Herb Stuffing

Cranberry-Port Conserve (page 10)

Grandma Wynn's Old-Fashioned
Cranberry Relish

Simple Grilled Fennel

Carrot and Sweet Potato Puree

*

Individual
Orange-Ginger Trifles

By now it seems that the past month has been one long whirl of gathering, making, decorating, and all the rest of the holiday busyness, so now it's time to sit down, relax, and enjoy the fruits of all the preparations. And what better way than to light the fire, gather a small but convivial group together for a quiet dinner that doesn't require too much work, some nice wine, and some good conversation with holiday music playing in the background.

Getting Ready The main course needs to be cooked just before serving, but much of the other preparation can be done a day or more in advance.

The soup can be made up to three weeks in advance and frozen, or make it a day in advance and reheat it just before serving. The two cranberry condiments are best made at least a few days before they're to be served. The crackers, too, can be made up to a week in advance and stored in tins.

Most of the preparation for the stuffing can

The table features a centerpiece of candles and a gathering of colorful ornaments. The printed napkins are from the fifties.
On the mantel, fresh greens are accented by dried hydrangeas, clusters of shiny balls, and chenille poinsettias from the forties.

be done a day in advance but the chicken breasts should be stuffed just before being put into the oven, about 1½ hours or so before before serving.

The carrot and sweet potato puree can be made a day ahead, if necessary, and reheated. The fennel is best prepared no sooner than early on the day it is to be served, but the preparation takes very little time.

The pound cake for the trifles can be made well in advance and frozen and the custard can be made a day in advance. Assemble the trifles no sooner than early in the day.

Brussels Sprout and Hazelnut Soup

* * *

SERVES 6 TO 8

3 tablespoons unsalted butter
2 medium onions, chopped
2 shallots, chopped
1 celery stalk, chopped
1 10-ounce carton Brussels sprouts
¼ cup chopped hazelnuts, lightly toasted
2 large baking potatoes, peeled and
    coarsely chopped
1 bay leaf
2 tablespoons parsley leaves
4 cups chicken or vegetable stock
½ cup milk
1 cup half-and-half or plain yogurt
Pinch of nutmeg
Salt and white pepper
Chives, for garnish

1. In a large, heavy saucepan, melt the butter over medium-low heat, then add the onions, shallots, and celery. Sauté until the onion is softened and transparent, about 7 minutes (do not allow to brown).

2. Meanwhile, trim the stem ends of the sprouts and chop them roughly into quarters. Add all the remaining ingredients except the half-and-half and seasonings and bring the mixture to a simmer.

3. Simmer the mixture until the sprouts are crisp-tender, about 7 minutes. Stir in the milk and half-and-half, then bring the mixture to just below simmering. In batches if necessary, transfer the mixture to a blender or the bowl of a food processor fitted with the steel chopping blade and process until very smooth. Season to taste with nutmeg, salt, and white pepper. (*The soup can be made a day in advance and refrigerated or made up to 3 weeks in advance and frozen. Reheat the soup over very low heat before serving.*)

4. Ladle the hot soup into individual bowls and garnish with chives. Serve immediately.

Parmesan Crackers

* * *

MAKES ABOUT 3 DOZEN CRACKERS

2 cups unbleached all-purpose flour
1 teaspoon salt
½ teaspoon ground white pepper
½ teaspoon baking powder
¼ cup (½ stick) cold unsalted butter
¾ cup freshly grated Parmesan cheese
½ cup milk
1 large egg, lightly beaten

1. In a mixing bowl, combine the flour, salt, white pepper, and baking powder and mix well. Using a pastry blender or 2 knives, cut in the butter and ¼ cup of the cheese until the mixture resembles coarse meal.

2. Add the milk and the egg and mix to form a stiff dough. Knead in the bowl until smooth. Divide the dough into 2 portions.

3. Preheat the oven to 400°F. Lightly grease baking sheets.

4. On a lightly floured surface, roll out one portion of the dough to a thickness of ⅛ inch, then sprinkle half the remaining cheese over the dough. Using a floured round biscuit cutter or a star-shaped cookie cutter, cut out the dough (or cut the dough into diamond shapes with a knife). Place the dough cutouts on a prepared baking sheet about 1 inch apart. Repeat with the remaining dough.

5. Bake until the edges of the crackers are nicely browned, about 10 minutes, then transfer the crackers to wire racks to cool. Pack the cooled crackers in wax paper-lined tins and store up to 3 weeks.

Roasted Chicken Breasts with Pear, Scallion, and Herb Stuffing

* * *

SERVES 6 TO 8

When making chicken breasts I always figure on about 1½ breast halves per person. When time for seconds rolls around, some guests will eat only one but some, for sure, will eat two.

> *5 whole chicken breasts, halved and*
> *   boned, with skin left on*
> *Pear, Scallion, and Herb Stuffing (recipe*
> *   follows)*
> *Whole sage leaves*
> *Salt and freshly ground black pepper*

1. Preheat the oven to 375°F. Lightly oil a shallow roasting pan or baking dish large enough to hold the rolled chicken breasts in one layer.

2. One at a time, place a chicken breast half on

Star-shaped Parmesan Crackers are served alongside this creamy Brussels Sprout and Hazelnut Soup.

a work surface skin-side up. Carefully loosen the skin along one side, then spoon 2 to 3 tablespoons of the stuffing under the skin and press to spread it evenly over the chicken. Tuck a sage leaf under the skin and over the stuffing, then turn the ends of the chicken under, forming a rounded roll. Place the rolls, skin-side up, in the baking pan. Season lightly with salt and pepper.

3. Bake, basting occasionally with the pan juices, until the chicken is cooked through and golden brown, 40 to 45 minutes. (*The chicken can be prepared a day in advance and stored, well wrapped, in the refrigerator, or freeze the fully cooked and tightly wrapped chicken for up to 2 weeks. Reheat in a 325°F. oven.*) Remove the pan from the oven, cover loosely with foil, and let stand for 10 or 15 minutes before serving.

A colorful main course featuring chicken breasts and Cranberry-Port Conserve (page 10) looks great on plain white plates.

Pear, Scallion, and Herb Stuffing

* * *

MAKES ABOUT 6 CUPS

*U*sing fresh herbs and pears rather than the more usual apples gives this stuffing a subtle flavor surprise without upsetting the holiday traditionalists.

½ cup (1 stick) unsalted butter
1 bunch (6 to 8) scallions, white and green parts, thinly sliced
1 medium onion, chopped
1 celery stalk, chopped
2 firm, ripe Bosc pears, pared and chopped
10 cups coarse, soft, fresh bread crumbs, lightly toasted

½ teaspoon salt
1 teaspoon coarsely ground black pepper
2 tablespoons chopped sage or 2 teaspoons dried rubbed sage
1 tablespoon thyme leaves or 1½ teaspoons dried thyme
1 tablespoon rosemary leaves or 1½ teaspoons dried rosemary, crumbled
¼ cup chopped parsley
1 cup chicken stock, approximately
2 large eggs, lightly beaten

1. Melt the butter in a large skillet over medium heat. Add the scallions, onion, and celery and sauté until the onion is transparent and golden, about 10 minutes. Stir in the pears.

2. Transfer the mixture to a large bowl and add the bread crumbs, salt, pepper, herbs, and stock and mix well. (*The mixture can be prepared several hours in advance and stored, covered, in the refrigerator; return to room temperature before proceeding.*) Add the eggs and mix well. Add a little more stock if the mixture seems too dry.

3. Use the stuffing to stuff the Roasted Chicken Breasts (page 81) and place the remaining stuffing in a lightly greased small baking dish, cover with foil, and bake in a 350°F. oven for 1 hour.

Grandma Wynn's Old-Fashioned Cranberry Relish

* * *

MAKES ABOUT 3 CUPS

This recipe appeared in my first book, *The Holidays,* and to those who already have it, my apologies; but I can never let the season go by without making a batch or two of this relish. It's not only tasty and pretty, but it's one of the easiest recipes in the world. The relish can be made in the food processor, but I prefer the texture that comes from using a hand-cranked food grinder like the one Grandma had.

1 medium orange
½ lemon
1 medium apple
3 cups (1 12-ounce bag) cranberries
½ cup sugar
¼ teaspoon ground cloves

1. Quarter the orange and lemon and remove the seeds. Quarter the apple and core it. Do not peel the fruit.

2. Grind all the fruit in a food grinder (or pulse-process in the bowl of a food processor until just finely ground). Stir in the sugar and cloves. Transfer the relish to a jar, cover tightly, and refrigerate at least 2 days before using.

Simple Grilled Fennel

* * *

SERVES 6 TO 8

Fennel is a vegetable that we tend to forget about, but it's especially tasty and beautiful when grilled or broiled. I make this ahead and serve it at room temperature.

2 to 3 tablespoons extra virgin olive oil
3 fennel bulbs, cut lengthwise into quarters
Salt and freshly ground black pepper
½ cup chicken stock
½ lemon

1. Preheat the broiler.

2. Using 1 tablespoon of the olive oil, lightly grease a large, shallow, flameproof baking dish. Arrange the fennel in a single layer, slightly overlapping the ends if necessary for it all to fit in the dish. Season with salt and plenty of pepper.

3. Brush the surface of the fennel with oil, then drizzle the chicken stock over all. Place the pan under the broiler and broil until the fennel is crisp-tender and the edges are just beginning to char (timing depends on the individual broiler).

4. Remove the pan from the heat, squeeze the lemon over the fennel, and allow the fennel to cool, then cover tightly and refrigerate up to 24 hours. Bring to room temperature before serving.

Carrot and Sweet Potato Puree

* * *

SERVES 6 TO 8

I love sweet potatoes, but I'm not a big fan of those holiday concoctions that are all gooey with marshmallows and brown sugar. Here, the natural sweetness of sweet potatoes and carrots complement each other quite nicely without any further ado.

> *3 sweet potatoes, peeled and cut into chunks*
> *Salt*
> *3/4 pound carrots, peeled and cut into chunks*
> *1 small onion, coarsely chopped*
> *2 tablespoons unsalted butter*
> *1/4 cup chicken or vegetable stock*
> *1 tablespoon brandy (optional)*
> *1/4 teaspoon grated nutmeg*

1. Place the sweet potatoes in a large pan with salted water to cover. Place over medium-high heat and bring to a boil. Reduce the heat to low and simmer until the potatoes are very tender, about 30 minutes.

2. Place the carrots and onion in a large pan with salted water to cover. Place over medium-high heat and bring to a boil. Reduce the heat to low and simmer until the carrots are very tender, about 30 minutes.

3. Drain the vegetables and, in batches, process them in a food processor to form a slightly lumpy puree.

4. Transfer the pureed vegetables to a large bowl, add the butter, stock, brandy, and nutmeg and using a wooden spoon, beat until well blended. (*To make the puree in advance, mound it into a baking dish, cover tightly with plastic wrap, and refrigerate up to 24 hours. Return to room temperature, then reheat, loosely covered, in a microwave oven or in a conventional oven at 350°F. for 30 to 40 minutes.*) Serve hot.

Individual Orange-Ginger Trifles

* * *

MAKES 8

Custard
3 1/2 cups milk
6 large egg yolks
1/2 cup sugar
1/4 teaspoon salt
1 1/2 teaspoons vanilla extract

Assembly
1 loaf Ginger Pound Cake (page 73)
3/4 cup best-quality orange marmalade
1/2 cup white rum, approximately
1/2 cup Grand Marnier liqueur, approximately
Lightly toasted sliced almonds
2 cups (1 pint) heavy cream
1/4 cup chopped preserved ginger, for garnish

1. Pour the milk into the top of a double boiler over simmering water and bring to just below the simmering point.

2. While the milk is heating, combine the egg yolks, sugar, and salt together in a mixing bowl and whisk vigorously until the yolks thicken slightly and lighten in color. Gradually whisk the hot milk into this mixture, whisking continuously.

3. Pour the combined mixture into the top of the double boiler and cook, stirring constantly, until the mixture is thick and coats the back of the spoon. (Be patient; sometimes this takes up to 10 minutes.) Do not let the mixture simmer at any point.

4. Have ready a large bowl filled halfway with ice. Remove the top of the double boiler from the heat and place it in the bowl. Add the vanilla and stir or whisk the custard briskly for 5 minutes to cool it off rapidly. Pour the custard into a bowl, place plastic wrap directly onto the surface of the custard, and cool completely. Refrigerate until needed.

5. Using about ¾ of the cake loaf, cut off the crusts (save the crusts and the end of the loaf as a snack for the cook!), then cut the cake horizontally into quarters. Spread the top of each layer with orange marmalade, then reassemble the cake. Cut the cake into ½-inch-thick slices, then cut each slice into fourths.

6. Have ready 8 large footed glasses or dessert dishes. Working carefully, loosely line the bottoms and sides of the glasses with the cake "sandwiches," then drizzle the cake generously with rum and Grand Marnier. Spoon some of the chilled custard into the lined glasses, add cubes of the remaining cake, a sprinkling of almonds, drizzle a little rum and Grand Marnier over the cake, and top with the remaining custard.

7. Cover the trifles with plastic wrap and refrigerate until ready to serve. Whip the cream until soft peaks form. Remove the covering from the trifles and mound the cream onto them. Sprinkle additional almonds and preserved ginger over the cream and serve.

Cream-topped, custardy trifle is one of those really, really rich desserts that I reserve for special occasions.

A Christmas Buffet Dinner

MENU FOR 10 TO 12

Old English Spiced Beef Roast

An Assortment of Mustards

Kentucky Turnip Pudding

*Brussels Sprout Salad
with Maple-Walnut Dressing*

Roasted Carrots and Green Beans

*

Fruited Ricotta Cheesecake

Apple-Walnut Torte

Chocolate Velvet Cake

Mom's side of the family is Welsh, so there's always been some of the British traditions in our holiday celebrations. This menu features a wonderful traditional Old English Spiced Beef Roast along with a few of my own favorite wintertime flavors. Note that there's plenty of dessert!

For big holiday dinners, I used to worry about having something that kids would like. For example, last Christmas we had goose for dinner and I was worried that my young niece and nephew might not like it, so I made a ham as well. Well, my adventuresome nephew Jared ate goose with enthusiasm and my more timid niece Amanda didn't touch either goose or ham (newborn niece Grace dozed on, exhibiting no interest at all!). And guess who got stuck eating ham for a week!

GETTING READY This is not a complicated menu to prepare, though some planning needs to be done to begin preparation of the beef.

Four days before Christmas, start marinating the beef; it will be finished on Christmas Eve day. The desserts can also be made a few days in advance. Store the cheesecake and chocolate cake in the refrigerator.

All the vegetables are best made the day they are served, but they can all be made a day in advance if need be.

It may be cold and snowy outside, but it's cozy in my farmhouse dining room. The table is set with inexpensive Christmas dishes with a selection from my Santa collection and bright red candles for a center-piece. The chandelier is decorated with greens.

The main course features a traditional Old English beef roast, which looks spectacular layered on a big ironstone platter gar-nished lavishly with fresh big sprigs of rosemary and kumquats.

Old English Spiced Beef Roast

* * *

SERVES 10 TO 12

This is an especially festive dish that makes a grand appearance on the Christmas buffet table. During Elizabethan times, when this method of curing and roasting beef was developed, the purpose was to preserve the beef, and the meat was cured for a week or more. This modern-day adaptation is cured just long enough for the seasonings to impart a rich flavor.

There are a few steps here, but the big plus is that the beef can be completely prepared a day before serving; rewarm it in a slow oven or serve it at room temperature. Just remember to start making this four days before serving.

Serve the beef with gherkins and a variety of mustards, such as hot English mustard, black mustard, and a grainy French one.

For Curing
About 6 pounds bottom round of beef (two 3- to 4-pound pieces)
1 teaspoon whole cloves
1 teaspoon ground mace
2 teaspoons whole allspice berries
2 tablespoons black peppercorns
1 tablespoon thyme leaves or 1½ teaspoons dried thyme
1 tablespoon rosemary leaves or 1½ teaspoons dried rosemary
4 bay leaves
2 tablespoons salt
¼ cup dark brown sugar
Rind of 1 orange, white part removed
3 large garlic cloves, crushed
1 cup dry red wine
¼ cup olive oil

For Roasting
2 large carrots, coarsely chopped
2 celery stalks with leaves, coarsely chopped
2 medium onions, coarsely chopped
3 large garlic cloves, crushed
1 cup well-seasoned beef stock
1 cup dry red wine

For Serving
Herb sprigs
Kumquats

1. Place the beef in a roasting pan just large enough to hold it comfortably.

2. In a coffee grinder or spice grinder, or with a mortar and pestle, combine the spices, thyme, rosemary, bay leaves, salt, sugar, and orange rind and grind until fine.

3. Place this mixture in a bowl and add the garlic, wine, and oil. Stir well, then pour this marinade over the beef. Cover the pan with foil and refrigerate for 3 days, turning once or twice a day.

4. The day before serving, preheat the oven to 300°F. Remove the beef from the pan, rinse it under cold running water to remove the curing seasonings, and pat it dry with paper towels. Wipe out the pan.

5. Arrange the carrots, celery, onions, and garlic evenly in the bottom of the pan, then place the meat on top. Pour the stock and wine over the meat. Cover the pan tightly with its lid or with foil. Place in the oven and roast until the meat is quite tender, about 4 hours.

6. Remove the pan to a wire rack and allow the meat to cool. Remove the beef from the pan and wrap it tightly. Place the roasts in the refrigerator between 2 cutting boards and weight down the top board. Chill the meat overnight.

7. Remove the roasts from the refrigerator. Cut the meat into thin slices and reassemble the slices to resemble a single roast. Wrap tightly with foil and refrigerate until an hour or so before serving. (*The wrapped roasts can also be returned to the pan and rewarmed in a 300°F. oven for about 40 minutes.*)

8. Arrange the meat on a large platter and decorate lavishly with herbs and a few kumquats.

Kentucky Turnip Pudding

* * *

SERVES 8 TO 10

Last fall, when I was appearing at the Kentucky Book Fair in the capital city of Frankfort, a few of us went on a hunt for some good local home-style cooking for dinner. We ended up at Ken-Tex, a barbecue drive-in, where spread before us was a buffet with all those wonderful down-home sides. We didn't have to choose among the green beans boiled forever with salt pork, the baked macaroni and cheese, perfection salad, corn bread stuffing, black-eyed peas, and all the rest; we just tasted a little of everything (the barbecue was great too).

One of the sides that I liked the best was this turnip pudding. I asked how it was made and was graciously given the "little of this, some of that" method for making it. When I got home I figured it out and here it is. (P.S. Even people who "hate" turnips like this pudding!)

4 cups white turnips (about 2 pounds),
    peeled and cut into chunks
3 cups boiling potatoes (about 1½
    pounds), peeled and cut into chunks
3 tablespoons unsalted butter, melted
¼ cup milk
2 teaspoons sugar
½ teaspoon salt
¼ teaspoon white pepper
2 large eggs, lightly beaten
¼ cup grated Parmesan cheese

1. Preheat the oven to 375°F. Lightly butter a shallow 1½-quart baking dish.

2. Combine the turnips and potatoes in a large pot with salted water to cover. Place over medium-high heat and bring to a boil. Reduce the heat to medium-low and boil until the vegetables are tender, about 20 minutes. Drain the vegetables, return them to the pot, and mash them, leaving them slightly lumpy.

3. In a small bowl, beat the remaining ingredients except for 2 tablespoons of the Parmesan cheese together with a fork. Add this mixture and mix until all the ingredients are just blended; the mixture should still be somewhat lumpy. Spoon the mixture into the prepared baking dish, leaving the surface somewhat "hilly," and sprinkle the remaining Parmesan over all. (*The pudding can be prepared up to this point early in the day. Cover and refrigerate, then return to room temperature before proceeding.*)

4. Bake until the pudding is puffed and the surface is nicely browned, 25 to 30 minutes. Serve hot.

Brussels Sprout Salad with Maple-Walnut Dressing

* * *

SERVES 8 TO 10

Dressing

¼ cup white wine vinegar
1 tablespoon prepared Dijon mustard
1 large garlic clove, crushed
1 tablespoon maple syrup
¼ cup olive oil
¼ cup walnut oil (if unavailable,
    additional olive oil can be substituted)

3 10-ounce cartons Brussels sprouts
¼ cup chopped walnuts, lightly toasted

Lots of side dishes are essential for a big holiday dinner.
At each place is a tiny fake tree trimmed with candies.

1. Combine the dressing ingredients in a jar, cover tightly, and shake until well blended. Let stand 1 hour, then remove the garlic clove.

2. Meanwhile, trim the ends of the Brussels sprouts, then score an X into each end. Remove any tough outer leaves and wash well under cold water to remove any sandy particles.

3. Place the sprouts in a vegetable steamer and steam over simmering water until crisp-tender, 7 to 10 minutes. Transfer the sprouts to a bowl, pour the dressing and chopped walnuts over them, and gently toss. Serve the salad warm or at room temperature. (*The salad can be prepared up to a day in advance and refrigerated; allow to come to room temperature before serving.*)

Roasted Carrots and Green Beans

* * *

SERVES 6 TO 8

*R*oasting vegetables with a little olive oil and garlic gives them a wonderfully rich flavor. They're great for a company dinner since they don't need much watching or fussing with.

1 pound carrots, peeled
4 garlic cloves, crushed
¼ cup extra virgin olive oil
¼ cup chicken or vegetable stock
1 pound green beans, stemmed
Salt and freshly ground black pepper

1. Preheat the oven to 375°F.

2. Cut the carrots into julienne about the length and width of the green beans. Place the vegetables in a large, shallow roasting pan; add the garlic, oil, and stock and toss to coat the carrots. Place the pan in the oven and bake until the carrots are tender and the beans are crisp-tender, about 1½ hours. Season to taste with salt and plenty of pepper.

Fruited Ricotta Cheesecake

* * *

MAKES ONE 8-INCH ROUND CAKE

A classic Italian version of cheesecake is lightly flavored with lemon and nutmeg and studded with candied peel.

Crust
¾ cup all-purpose flour
3 tablespoons granulated sugar
⅓ cup unsalted butter
1 large egg yolk, lightly beaten
½ teaspoon vanilla extract

Filling
3 cups lowfat ricotta cheese
½ cup granulated sugar
¼ cup milk
¼ cup unbleached all-purpose flour
½ teaspoon salt
¼ teaspoon grated nutmeg
3 large eggs
1 tablespoon rum or 1 teaspoon rum
    extract
3 tablespoons chopped candied orange peel
3 tablespoons chopped candied lemon peel
3 tablespoons golden raisins
Grated rind of 1 small lemon
Confectioners' sugar, for dusting

1. Preheat the oven to 350°F.

2. In a mixing bowl, stir the flour and granulated sugar together, then using 2 knives or a pastry blender, cut in the butter. Stir in the egg yolk and vanilla, mixing until the dough is just moistened. Press the dough into the bottom and sides of an 8-inch springform pan.

3. Place the pan in the oven and bake until the crust just begins to turn golden, 5 to 7 minutes. Remove the pan from the oven and set aside.

4. To make the filling, combine the ricotta, sugar, milk, flour, salt, and nutmeg in a mixing bowl and beat until smooth, then beat in the eggs and rum. Stir in the candied peels and lemon rind.

5. Pour the filling into the prebaked crust. Place the pan on a small baking sheet and bake the cake until the edges are nicely browned and the center is firm to the touch, about 45 minutes.

6. Place the cake pan on a wire rack to cool for 20 minutes. Using a table knife, carefully loosen the sides of the crust from the pan, then let the cake cool for 20 minutes more before removing the outside ring from the pan.

7. Once the cake is completely cooled, replace the outside ring to protect the cake. Cover the pan with foil or plastic wrap and chill for 3 hours or overnight. (*The cake can be made up to 2 days in advance of serving.*) Remove the outer ring from the pan, carefully separate the cake from the bottom of the pan with a spatula, and slide the cake onto a platter or cake stand.

8. Dust the surface of the cake lightly with confectioners' sugar and decorate with orange slices.

Apple-Walnut Torte

* * *

MAKES ONE 10-INCH ROUND CAKE

*H*ere's an all-purpose cake that can be served as dessert after dinner, at breakfast, or as a late-night snack.

1 cup sugar
½ cup (1 stick) unsalted butter, softened
2 large eggs
1 teaspoon vanilla extract
1 cup unbleached all-purpose flour
1 teaspoon baking powder
¼ teaspoon salt
¾ cup finely chopped walnuts

2 Granny Smith apples, peeled, pared,
  and thinly sliced
1 teaspoon ground cinnamon
2 tablespoons unsalted butter, melted
Whipped cream, for garnish

1. Preheat the oven to 350°F. Lightly grease a 10-inch springform pan.

2. In a mixing bowl, cream ¾ cup of the sugar and the butter, then beat in the eggs and vanilla. In a separate bowl, sift together the flour, baking powder, and salt, then beat the dry mixture into the wet mixture. Stir in ½ cup walnuts.

3. Spread the dough evenly in the prepared pan. Arrange the apple slices on top of the batter in two slightly overlapping circles.

4. In the small bowl, combine the remaining ¼ cup almonds, the remaining ¼ cup sugar, and the cinnamon. Sprinkle this mixture over the batter then drizzle the melted butter over all.

5. Bake until a cake tester or wooden pick inserted in the center comes out clean, about 1 hour. Serve the cake warm (if made in advance, reheat in a low oven), cut into thin wedges. Top each serving with a dollop of whipped cream and a few of the remaining sliced almonds.

Chocolate Velvet Cake

* * *

MAKES ONE 9-INCH ROUND CAKE

*T*his simple chocolate cake with a subtle orange flavor can be served either plain or fancy as in the variation at the end of the recipe and the photograph on the opposite page.

⅓ cup unbleached all-purpose flour
1 teaspoon ground cinnamon
½ cup (1 stick) unsalted butter, softened
1 cup granulated sugar
6 large eggs, separated
1 teaspoon vanilla extract
8 ounces unsweetened chocolate, melted
  and cooled
⅓ cup ground almonds
1 teaspoon grated orange rind

1. Preheat the oven to 350°F. Lightly grease a 9-inch springform pan.

2. In a small bowl, stir the flour and cinnamon together until well blended. Set aside.

3. In a mixing bowl, cream the butter and granulated sugar together until light and fluffy, then beat in the egg yolks and vanilla. Slowly beat in the chocolate, then beat in the almonds, flour-cinnamon mixture, and orange rind.

4. In a separate bowl, beat the egg whites until stiff peaks form. Fold about 1 cup of the chocolate mixture into the egg whites, then gently fold this mixture into the chocolate mixture.

5. Transfer the batter to the prepared pan and bake until the cake has set and a cake tester or wooden pick inserted in the center comes out clean, 60 to 65 minutes. Place the pan on a wire rack to cool. Cover the pan and store the cake in the refrigerator until an hour before serving.

6. To decorate, remove the cake from the pan and carefully slide it onto a serving plate. Place a paper doily on top of the cake, dust it with confectioners' sugar, and carefully remove the doily.

Berry-Glazed Chocolate Velvet Cake
Arrange an overlapping ring of sliced strawberries around the edge of the cooled cake, then cover the cake with raspberries. Glaze the berries with melted currant jelly, then chill the cake as above.

At Christmas, I like to have an assortment of desserts so everyone can have a favorite or sample a little of everything.

* * * * * * * * * * * *

Index

Conversion Chart
Equivalent Imperial and Metric Measurements

American cooks use standard containers, the 8-ounce cup and a tablespoon that takes exactly 16 level fillings to fill that cup level. Measuring by cup makes it very difficult to give weight equivalents, as a cup of densely packed butter will weigh considerably more than a cup of flour. The easiest way therefore to deal with cup measurements in recipes is to take the amount by volume rather than by weight. Thus the equation reads:

$$1 \text{ cup} = 240 \text{ ml} = 8 \text{ fl. oz.} \quad \tfrac{1}{2} \text{ cup} = 120 \text{ ml} = 4 \text{ fl. oz.}$$

It is possible to buy a set of American cup measures in major stores around the world.

In the States, butter is often measured in sticks. One stick is the equivalent of 8 tablespoons. One tablespoon of butter is therefore the equivalent to ½ ounce/15 grams.

Liquid Measures

Fluid ounces	U.S.	Imperial	Milliliters
	1 teaspoon	1 teaspoon	5
¼	2 teaspoon	1 dessert spoon	7
½	1 tablespoon	1 tablespoon	15
1	2 tablespoon	2 tablespoon	28
2	¼ cup	4 tablespoon	56
4	½ cup or ¼ pint		110
5		¼ pint or 1 gill	140
6	¾ cup		170
8	1 cup or ½ pint		225
9			250, ¼ liter
10	1¼ cups	½ pint	280
12	1½ cups	¾ pint	340
15	¾ pint		420
16	2 cups or 1 pint		450
18	2¼ cups		500, ½ liter
20	2½ cups	1 pint	560
24	3 cups or 1½ pints		675
25		1¼ pints	700
27	3½ cups		750
30	3¾ cups	1½ pints	840
32	4 cups or 2 pints or 1 quart		900
35		1¾ pints	980
36	4½ cups		1000, 1 liter
40	5 cups or 2½ pints	2 pints or 1 quart	1120
48	6 cups or 3 pints		1350
50		2½ pints	1400
60	7½ cups	3 pints	1680
64	8 cups or 4 pints or 2 quarts		1800
72	9 cups		2000, 2 liters

Solid Measures

U.S. and Imperial Measures		Metric Measures	
ounces	pounds	grams	kilos
1		28	
2		56	
3½		100	
4	¼	112	
5		140	
6		168	
8	½	225	
9		250	¼
12	¾	340	
16	1	450	
18		500	½
20	1¼	560	
24	1½	675	
27		750	¾
28	1¾	780	
32	2	900	
36	2¼	1000	1
40	2½	1100	
48	3	1350	
54		1500	1½
64	4	1800	
72	4½	2000	2
80	5	2250	2¼
90		2500	2½
100	6	2800	2¾

Oven Temperature Equivalents

Fahrenheit	Celsius	Gas Mark	Description
225	110	¼	Cool
250	130	½	
275	140	1	Very Slow
300	150	2	
325	170	3	Slow
350	180	4	Moderate
375	190	5	
400	200	6	Moderately Hot
425	220	7	Fairly Hot
450	230	8	Hot
475	240	9	Very Hot
500	250	10	Extremely Hot

Linear and Area Measures

1 inch	2.54 centimeters
1 foot	0.3048 meters
1 square inch	6.4516 square centimeters
1 square foot	929.03 square centimeters